THE RUSSIAN PH...

Francis House

The Russian Phoenix

THE STORY OF RUSSIAN CHRISTIANS
AD 998–1988

First published in Great Britain 1988
SPCK
Holy Trinity Church
Marylebone Road
London NW1 4DU

British Library Cataloguing in Publication Data

House, Francis
    The Russian phoenix: the story of Russian
    Christians AD 988–1988.
    1. Soviet Union — Church history
    I. Title
    274.7   BR932
    ISBN 0–281–04341–8

Printed in Great Britain by
Latimer Trend & Company Ltd, Plymouth

For Margaret

Contents

Acknowledgements

I am most grateful to the bishops and theologians of the Moscow Patriarchate who have influenced my appreciation of the history of the Russian Church, but after so many years I cannot now identify all my sources, and the judgements are my own. I am particularly indebted to Professor Leo Zander of the Institute of St Sergius in Paris, to Dr Paul Anderson, the expert on Orthodox affairs of the YMCA and the American Episcopal Church, to Dr Nicolas Zernov, founder of the Fellowship of St Alban and St Sergius and for many years Spalding Lecturer in the University of Oxford, to Sir John Lawrence, and to the Reverend Michael Bourdeaux and the staff of Keston College. The Reverend Dr Sergei Hackel kindly read the draft of Chapters 1–5 and 7–9, and the Reverend Dr David Russell CBE read Chapters 6 and 10. Lists of sources and suggestions for further reading are appended. I take responsibility personally for all misinterpretations and errors of fact.

Thanks are also due to the following for permission to use the photographs reproduced in this book:

The Moscow Patriarchate: pp. 60, 69, 71, 77, 80, 93, 97, 117; colour section pp. 4, 5 (top), 6–7.

Aid to the Persecuted (formerly Underground Evangelism): colour section pp. 3 (top), 8 (top and centre).

Keston College: pp. 99, 110.

The World Council of Churches: colour section p. 5 (bottom).

John Innes: p. 4

John Thorne: colour section p. 8 (bottom).

Francis House: p. 88; colour section pp. 1, 2, 3 (bottom).

Introduction

In 1988 Russian Christians are publicly celebrating the 'Baptism of Rus' a thousand years ago. Many visitors report that churches are overcrowded. Some Western experts estimate that there are at least thirty million regular Christian worshippers in the USSR. Soviet officials and Russian churchmen frequently affirm that 'Religion is free'.

But such statements are greeted with scepticism in the West. Many Christians and secular journalists doubt whether genuine Churches still exist. Amnesty International, Keston College and other well-informed agencies constantly publish reports of Christians being imprisoned or sent to penal work-camps or internal exile.

Where does the truth lie?

Several well-documented studies of the religious situation have been published in the West. These often reproduce *samizdat* material which circulates secretly in the USSR. This frequently contradicts official pronouncements. And there are deep divisions among Western students. Some believe that Russian Christians who suffer harassment, imprisonment and exile represent the only true Church. Others take more sympathetic views of those who have reached some kind of accommodation with the atheistic Communist Party–State. It is not surprising that ordinary Western observers are often bewildered and sceptical.

In fact many of the causes of the present state of affairs date back to long before 1917. The story of Russian Christians in the past can illuminate the present. Unfortunately Russia has been culturally isolated for so long that few Westerners know anything of its history. But there is much that is relevant and inspiring as well as informative in the costly witness of the Russian Churches, especially in their Phoenix-like resurrections from disaster and oppression.

Many different national religious groups exist within the USSR. Christians include Armenians, Lithuanian Roman Catholics, Latvian Lutherans and others. The distinctive traditions of each of these groups deserve to be better known. But this story is primarily concerned with Russian

ix

Christians belonging to the Orthodox or Baptist–Evangelical Churches.

I am not a member of the Orthodox Church, but I write as one who has learnt to appreciate and love many aspects of Orthodoxy. My understanding of the Christian faith has been greatly enriched by Orthodox friends and teachers, and I believe that my fellow-Anglicans and Western Christians generally have much to learn from the Russian experience.

FRANCIS HOUSE
September 1987

PART ONE

The Russian Churches before the Revolution

1
The Baptism of Rus

Most days a long queue snakes across the Red Square in
Moscow. Most foreign visitors have seen it. Numbers of
Russian tourists visiting the capital join it. Their goal is the
chief shrine of Soviet Russia: the tomb in which Lenin's
body lies embalmed. The whole scene evokes memories of
centuries of Russian history. The huge granite cube of the
Soviet mausoleum stands out against the rose-coloured
brickwork of the medieval fortifications of the Kremlin. In
the background rise the fantastic cupolas of the cathedral of
St Basil, which was built to celebrate the final Russian
victory over the Tatars four hundred years ago.

A foreigner who joins the queue will be kindly pushed
forward to the front. Soon he comes to the sentries, magnifi-
cently attired in winter from head to foot in bearskins.
Passing through a dimly lit passage he enters a small hall
suffused with yellow light. There in a glass case Lenin's
body lies. The atmosphere in the chamber is somewhat
oppressive. But the Russian tourists relax in cheerful conversation once they have passed the guards on the other side.
They have done their duty as good citizens of the Communist state.

The priority given to visits to Lenin's tomb is a reminder
that from the first his policy was to deprive the Church of
any influence on government or people. He believed that
Marxist materialism would inevitably replace Christianity as
the working 'faith' of the Russian people and he sought to
accelerate the process. The persecution in the twenty years
which followed the Bolshevik revolution was proportion-
ately more severe than the persecutions suffered by the early
Church under the Roman Empire. After Lenin's death the
'Lenin cult' was deliberately introduced as an alternative to
religious faith.

However, on the occasion of the Orthodox Christmas, and

more especially on Easter Eve, Moscow witnesses very different scenes. Then the streets and squares round the forty-three 'working' churches are crammed with many thousands of worshippers. Independent observers from France, Germany and Britain agree that something like twenty per cent of the adult population of European Russia still openly attend churches at least from time to time, and it is impossible to know how many more thousands of men and women, young as well as old, are 'crypto-Christians', believers who pray secretly although they have strong family or professional reasons for concealing their beliefs for the time being (e.g. until their children have grown up and will no longer suffer hostility and deprivation because their parents are known to be believers). So seventy years after the 'October Revolution' the Orthodox Church still maintains a visible presence in the professedly atheistic Soviet state. To explain this paradox it is advisable to look back all the way to AD 988, the year in which the Russian state officially adopted Christianity.

The actual 'Baptism of the Russians' must have been very like the first baptisms of the English three centuries earlier.

The baptism of Prince Vladimir

4

In both cases missionaries from a faraway Church were welcomed by the rulers of Kent or Northumbria or Kiev. In both cases, following the conversion of the prince, hundreds of ordinary citizens followed their leaders down into nearby rivers or streams for baptism in the primitive style by total immersion in the waters. (St Paul eloquently described such baptisms as symbolizing spiritual death and resurrection.) Missionary priests were few and pre-baptismal instruction must have been minimal; but in each case the spectacular scenes in the rivers marked a new beginning. The old gods were put away. The people followed their rulers in a new commitment to what was in principle a universal faith rather than a local cult. In both cases acceptance of the Christian faith opened up contacts with an older and richer culture. But there was one major difference: the English were baptized into what became the Western, the Russians into the Eastern, Church.

How was it that Prince Vladimir of Kiev came to seek baptism for himself and for his people? Who indeed were these princes of Kiev? Strangely enough they were cousins of the heathen Vikings who were savagely pillaging Christian England in that very year 988. The Scandinavian princes known as the Varangians had come to Russia a century earlier not as conquerors but at the invitation of the Russians themselves. According to the tradition recorded by the chroniclers they came to power not like William the Conqueror, by invasion, but at the request of the citizens of the divided and disorganized small Russian city-states. 'Our land is great and rich,' they were said to have told the Varangians, 'but there is no order in it. Come to rule over us!' So the ancestors of Prince Vladimir came to rule over a vast domain stretching from south of Kiev, six hundred miles north to where Leningrad now stands, and five hundred miles from east to west, from the Volga to what became the Polish border.

The Scandinavian rulers married Russian wives and soon adopted Slavonic names. By 988 Prince Vladimir was no longer regarded as a foreigner. The chroniclers tell us that he had decided to strengthen the bonds between the town-dwellers and tribal peoples of his enormous country by the adoption of a single religion. As a pagan he is said to have devoutly offered hundreds of human sacrifices to the local gods, but it became clear to him that a 'world religion' would have more power to integrate and civilize his people. But which religion was it to be? Judaism, Islam or Christianity? And if Christianity, should it be Roman Catholicism or Eastern Orthodoxy? A medieval Russian legend has it that the Prince sent deputations to examine all four possibilities. Judaism was rejected because, although there were Jews everywhere, they were only scattered minorities without political power. Islam was rejected on the very practical grounds that it would be very hard to survive the Russian winter without alcohol. Roman Catholicism was probably rejected because it would involve the subjection of the Russian princes to the pope.

But the delegation sent to Constantinople returned convinced that Orthodoxy would serve them best. The highlight of their visit had been attendance at a celebration of the Holy Liturgy by the Patriarch in the magnificent church of the Holy Wisdom, St Sophia. The Russians were said to have been so transported by the spiritual splendour of the service: by the lights, the incense, the vestments, the music and the glory of the architecture, that 'they did not know whether they were in heaven or on earth. They only knew that God dwells there among men. They could never forget that beauty.'

Whatever historical facts may lie behind this attractive legend, it is certain that for many centuries the approach to Christian faith through the beauty of worship has been a distinctive characteristic of Russian church life. In our own day a young Russian who was to become an outstanding if controversial leader in the Orthodox Church, had been brought up in a militantly atheistic family. He knew nothing of Christianity except what he had been taught in antireligious lessons at his school. But at the age of sixteen he happened to pass the open door of a church in which the Liturgy was being celebrated. He went in and was captivated by what he saw and heard. He became a secret worshipper, and as soon as he was eighteen he became a monk. (See page 92 below.)

The conversion of the Russians to Orthodoxy was also facilitated by the established missionary policy of the Eastern Church in accordance with which the liturgy, psalms and New Testament had already been translated into Slavonic some time before 988. A liturgy in their own language was more acceptable than the Latin of the Roman Church. But though the use of Slavonic initially helped the work of the Orthodox missionaries in Russia, over the following centuries its use also contributed to the isolation of the Russians from Western Europe. Very few Westerners learnt Russian, and during the centuries when Latin was the *lingua franca* of Europe, few Russians could speak it. Nicolas Zernov observed that 'the Russia of the Middle Ages was nurtured not on a Latin grammar or on Greek philosophy but on a Slavonic psalter'. This had one positive result – the relatively small influence of clericalism in the Russian Church. The Orthodox clergy remained closer to their congregations. In the West for the most part only the clergy knew Latin, but in Russia, Slavonic could be understood by any literate layman. Consequently there was much less danger of the clergy becoming a separate ruling caste. While in the West churchmen held many of the high offices of state, in Russia the clergy were as a rule regarded primarily as leaders of worship rather than as authorities in civilian life. (There were of course important exceptions.) The magnificence of the churches which survive from this early flowering of Christianity in Kiev and from subsequent centuries further north, testify to the supreme importance Russian rulers accorded to worship. The Orthodox Church in the Soviet Union today observes the same priorities.

Another characteristic which the contemporary Church in the USSR has inherited from those early days is an emphasis on martyrdom, the acceptance of suffering and identification with the poor. The first two saints 'canonized' in Russia were not monks or bishops but two young princes, Boris and Gleb, who were murdered by their elder brother in AD 1015. If they had decided to resist they might have had the support of their own bodyguards, but they declared that as Christians they would rather be killed than shed blood in self-defence. They have subsequently been commemorated as

7

'passion-bearers'. Icons painted in following centuries testify to their enduring attraction. (Their pacifist English contemporary, Edmund of East Anglia, King and Martyr, gained nothing like the same continuous popularity.)

Another early Russian saint, Theodosios, who died in 1074, was an exemplar of a distinctive feature of Russian monasticism. The son of a wealthy family, he insisted on joining his father's serfs in their work in the fields, wearing their clothes and sharing their poverty and humiliation. When his mother protested, he spoke of how 'our Lord Jesus Christ humbled himself and gave us an example'. When later he became an abbot, he built accommodation for the sick and destitute, and made his monastery a centre for penitence and spiritual guidance for the laity – a tradition which was powerfully revived by some Russian monasteries in the eighteenth and nineteenth centuries.

So the foundations of the Russian Church were well and truly laid at Kiev at about the time when the Norman kings were establishing their power in England. But while England was becoming steadily more rich and civilized, the culture of the great Duchy of Kiev was being undermined and eventually destroyed, first by the piratical Pechenegs who cut the vital trade-routes down the Dnieper to Constantinople, and then, soon afterwards, when destructive waves of Tatars swept across the country from the East.

2
Under the Tatar Yoke

Weakened by internal disorder, the loss of its lucrative transit trade and the lack of clear rules for the succession of its princes, Kiev was unable to put up any prolonged resistance to the mounted invaders from central Asia who attacked between 1223 and 1240. All the cities and towns of the Duchy, except Novgorod and Pskov in the far north-west, were sacked and burnt. Tens of thousands of Russians were killed or carried off as slaves. Most of the rest were driven from their homes and farms on the rich but indefensible 'black earth' of the Ukraine, and had to find refuge in the forest country further north in Central Russia. From that time right up to the fifties of the present century, the majority of the Russians lived in scattered villages often isolated from one another by winter snows and spring floods. (As late as 1943, flying at a low altitude from Astrakhan to Moscow, I was astonished by the enormous extent of uncultivated steppe and forest.)

For the next two hundred years the inhabitants of the small Russian towns which survived were forced to pay heavy annual tributes to their Tatar overlords who ruled from their great strongholds at Kazan and Sarai on the Volga. Even Alexander Nevski, subsequently regarded by the Church as a great martial saint and by Stalin as a national hero, had to make an act of abject submission to the great Khan and spent a year at his court. But having thus secured himself from attack from the east he became able to repel invaders from the west. First, in 1240, he defeated a powerful Swedish army on the banks of the Neva river. (Hence the title 'Nevski'.) Then only two years later he had to face still more formidable foes – the Teutonic Knights. They were a crusading order based in Prussia. Like the Latin crusaders who had captured Constantinople in 1204, they regarded the Orthodox as heretics. The object of their crusade was to replace the Orthodox clergy by bishops and clergy of the papal obedience, and of course to gain new lands and serfs for themselves. Their forces were spearheaded by squadrons of heavily armoured cavalry. (The film which the great Russian film producer Eisenstein made for Stalin just before the Nazi invasion in 1941 evokes a terrifying picture of military power resembling that of the Panzers.)

To many Russians in the thirteenth century the Knights must have seemed irresistible. But Alexander Nevski was a man of deep Christian faith and courage. The chronicler attributes to him this moving prayer:

> O Lord of truth and power, who dost order all nations to remain in their own dominions, and who dost fix their boundaries, look upon the plight of thy servants and give them strength to repel the invaders.

In the event a fierce battle was fought partly on the frozen waters of Lake Peipus. Many of the heavily-armoured Knights were drowned when the ice broke under their weight. Alexander's small army won the day against all the odds. The advance of the Latin crusaders was halted, and Orthodoxy continued to be the faith of the Russian people.

One of Alexander's few supporters in the policy of submission to Tatar suzerainty had been Cyril, Metropolitan of Kiev 1242–81. Nearly all the metropolitans appointed by the patriarch of Constantinople had been Greeks, but when large parts of the country had been devastated by the Mongols, no Greek was willing to accept appointment, so providentially the Patriarch chose a very able Russian. Despite their commitment to Islam, the Mongol rulers often looked to Orthodox bishops and clergy to keep order among the subject Christian populations. The higher clergy were given protection and certain privileges, but their continuation in office was dependent on the approval of their masters. Cyril made good use of his position to revive and maintain some vestige of national unity among the citizens of the small towns and principalities into which Russia was divided. They gave moral support to princes who took a longer and wider view of their responsibilities. And so they played a vital part in preparing the way for the emergence of a single

Russian state when at last the power of the Tatar Khans began to wane.

After the destruction of Kiev, the main centre of church life moved north to Vladimir on the edge of the forest belt between the rivers Volga and Oka. But Vladimir was not destined to become the capital of 'all the Russias'. That distinction was to come to what in 1147 was only an insignificant wooden fort strategically situated on the Moskva river in the very centre of the territories where most of the Russians now lived. Through tributary rivers and easy porterage, in an age when communications by water were vitally important, Moscow had connections with the Oka and the Volga to the north and east, with the Dnieper and Western Dvina to the west and south, and with rivers which flowed into the Baltic to the north-west.

So it came about that in 1263 Daniel, Alexander Nevski's youngest son, chose Moscow as the site of the capital of his small patrimony. He was a most adroit ruler who steadily increased the area of his domain by intrigue, purchase, the threat of force, and especially by the conclusion of treaties which gradually brought other petty princes under his control. During a reign of forty years he succeeded in doubling the size of his principality. So it was not surprising that from 1326 onwards the metropolitans of the Orthodox Church resided in Moscow as a place of stable government which was least likely to suffer from attacks by Tatars from the east or by the aggressive Roman Catholic rulers of Lithuania from the west. (The 'Danilov' monastery there is being restored in 1988.)

Moscow's slow rise to dominance continued under Daniel's successors – mostly by unheroic means. No other Russian princes were so assiduous in their attendance at the court of the Great Khan or more willing to join the Tatar armies in crushing insurrections by rival rulers. They were so successful in gaining the confidence of their overlords that they were granted the right to collect the taxes imposed by the Khans on all the Russian principalities, and in 1353 they were actually recognized by the Tatars as having judicial authority over all the other princes. At the same time people were flocking to Moscow because, like the metropolitans, they saw that life was more secure there. So geographical, political and ecclesiastical forces combined to increase Moscow's power, and in the second half of the fourteenth century, Prince Dmitri, described by the historian Sir Bernard Pares as Russia's 'Black Prince', was able to build up a league of princes for mutual assistance.

At the same time a group of monks were gathering round a hermit who lived in the forests fifty miles north-east of Moscow in a place then called Radonezh, now Zagorsk. The hermit's name was Sergius. By the time of his death in 1392 he had become widely known and revered. So when in 1380 an immense army of militantly Islamic Tatars advanced up the valley of the Don to crush a Russian rebellion, Sergius encouraged Prince Dmitri to resist. It was a very grave decision. The Supreme Khan of the Golden Horde had assembled Muslim soldiers from the whole area from the Caucasus and the Caspian to the Carpathians. He had secured the support of the Prince of Lithuania to the west, and the republic of Genoa provided his armies with military experts and the most modern weapons. The Russians had to stand alone against a force of 400,000 men bent on the destruction of their Church and their national identity.

When the Tatar army had already entered Muscovite territory and the much smaller Russian army was already assembling at Kolomna, south of Moscow, Prince Dmitri and his closest associates went to visit St Sergius. It was still possible for them to lay down their arms and plead for mercy. Defeat would mean the massacre of the population and the destruction of the Church. Submission would probably be followed by the execution of the princes and the moral collapse of the people. The odds against a Russian victory were very heavy. What would the saintly hermit advise?

Sergius lived the life of a simple peasant far from the seats of temporal power. He had usually remained detached from all political and military decisions. But on this occasion he gave a firm prophetic lead. He encouraged Dmitri to take what must have seemed to many the suicidal course of advancing southward and meeting the enemy on the open steppes. He gave the Prince his blessing and promised victory. He sent two monks who had formerly been soldiers to accompany Dmitri. But the Orthodox Church did not produce the type of soldier bishop or monk who led contemporary crusades in the Catholic West, and these monks went with the army exclusively in a spiritual role.

The next week the Russian army of 160,000 men, the largest ever assembled up to that time, marched south. When they were hesitating to cross the Don on to the steppe, a message came from Sergius: 'Have no doubts. Go forward with faith. Confront the foe's ferocity. Have no fear. God is on your side.' Thus encouraged Dmitri led his troops across the river.

The battle which settled the fate of the Russian nation, state and Church (and possibly of all Eastern Europe too) was fought on the field of Kulikovo on 8 September 1380. At first the smaller Russian forces were pushed back by sheer weight of numbers. The Tatar horsemen were launched on what they expected to be a victorious pursuit, but a small body of well-disciplined Russians who had been concealed in an ambush suddenly attacked them from the rear. Panic spread and by nightfall the mighty Tatar host was itself in flight.

Far away in his monastery, St Sergius is said to have foreseen the day of victory, and at the time when the battle was being most fiercely contested he called the monks together to pray for the souls of those who were being killed. It is one of the paradoxes of Russian history that the eventual liberation of the country from the Tatar yoke should have been inspired by a monk who had 'left the world' and given his life entirely to the glorification of the Holy Trinity.

But the cost of those centuries of subjection was very heavy. Western Christians remember the thirteenth and fourteenth centuries as the climax of the Middle Ages; the time when our ancestors were building our great cathedrals, founding universities, increasing in civilization and accumulating wealth. But it was Russia's fate to suffer under the Tatars during the same period. For two hundred and fifty years there was decline and degeneration in many ways. The towns lost most of their organs of self-government when numerous English towns were receiving their charters. The condition of the Russian peasants was tending more and more towards serfdom when English yeomen were becoming an ever stronger force in society. Until about 1450, when Andrei Rublev began painting marvellous icons, craftsmanship and artistry declined in Russia while the early Renaissance was flourishing in Western Europe. Religious and historical writings were scanty and poor with nothing to compare with what was being produced by Aquinas and Dante and the other great theologians, philosophers, poets and writers of France, Italy and England. And Russian women were liable to be subjected to Islam-like manners. So, while Western civilization was flourishing, Russia had been thrown back into the equivalent of the Dark Ages. The country was only finally delivered from Tatar rule in 1481, a hundred years after the battle of Kulikovo.

3
Moscow: the Third Rome

At the beginning of the sixteenth century Basil III of
Moscow and Henry VIII of England both faced similar
problems over the succession to their thrones. Neither
monarch had a son by his first wife. Both decided that they
must marry again. Both were confronted with ecclesiastics
who declared that divorce was unjustified because the wives
had committed no offence. Henry's solution was to repudiate
the authority of the Papacy. Basil succeeded in getting a
compliant bishop appointed as Metropolitan of Moscow.
Thereafter the stories diverge completely. Henry's only son
Edward died before he was sixteen; but Basil's son by his
second wife became the powerful monarch known to poster-
ity as 'Ivan the Terrible' or 'the Dread', who finally achieved
the conquest of the Tatar Khanate of Astrakhan in 1556, just
before Queen Elizabeth the First acceded to the English
throne.

The conflict over the succession in Moscow did not have
such drastic results as the Reformation in England;
nevertheless it was one incident in an internal church struggle which affected the relations of Church and state in Russia
for four hundred years. It might indeed be argued that the
current clash between the official leaders of the Russian
Church and those who are convinced that they have con-
ceded too much to the Communist rulers of the Kremlin
reflects this sixteenth-century division in the Church.

Two outstanding abbots led the two parties at that time.
The followers of St Nil of Sorsk (1433–1508) were known as
the 'non-possessors' because they believed that monasteries
should not own serfs or large estates, but that the monks
should be self-supporting. They denied the authority of the
state in spiritual questions and they opposed the use of
secular force to punish heretics. When the question of the
royal divorce came up they held to a strict interpretation of

Jesus' prohibition of divorce as recorded in St Mark's Gospel.

On the other side the followers of St Joseph of Volotsk (1440–1515) were known as the 'possessors', because they maintained that ownership of land and serfs by the monasteries was a legal practice approved by church tradition. They thought that monastic communities should be free to concentrate on their primary work of unceasing prayer combined with care for the poor and giving spiritual direction. For the proper discharge of these functions the monasteries needed to be adequately endowed with lands and labourers. They gave great weight to the teaching of the Old Testament that those who broke God's laws should be punished by the temporal rulers. On the question of the divorce they considered that the national importance of having a legitimate heir to the throne outweighed the rights of a childless wife.

Behind these differences over ecclesiastical policy there lay a still deeper division. The followers of St Nil laid emphasis on the personal relationship between God and every individual believer. As Nicolas Zernov observed, 'To them Christianity was the religion of love and freedom. They were essentially New Testament Christians.' They maintained the message of the prophets who proclaimed that God requires righteousness in individuals more than costly sacrifices or magnificent buildings. For them meditation, chastity, fasting and prayer were more important than elaborate worship.

The Josephians on the other hand emphasized the ritual sanctification of the whole life of the nation. They stressed the corporate life of the Church, the obligation of liturgical worship and the values of well-ordered monastic communities. They taught that every Christian home should be modelled on a monastery. The father of each family should lead daily worship at the icon-corner. The man should exercise absolute authority over his wife, children and servants. Every event in life should be sanctified by the rites of the Church, for example, by saying grace before and after meals. Above all, they believed that worship offered in the sanctuary according to the rules of the Fathers, cleansed individual and corporate sins, opened the gates of heaven and would bring peace to mankind. When in 1943 the future Patriarch Alexis told the Archbishop of York that the only essential function of the Church was to offer the Divine Liturgy he was speaking in that tradition.

In many respects the convictions of 'possessors' and 'non-possessors' can be recognized in historical perspective as being complementary; but in Moscow in the sixteenth century the conflict between the two parties was bitterly fought out. In accordance with their principles the Josephians used the powers of the state to arrest, imprison and exile many of St Nils' followers, and to impose their own views on Church and state alike. (May we not recall parallels in sixteenth- and seventeenth-century England and France?) But in Nicolas Zernov's judgement, 'in spite of the triumphs of the empire and the splendour of the life of the Church' in the period of their ascendancy, they were 'undermining the spiritual vitality of the Russian nation' and 'preparing the ground for the great schism of the Russian Church in the seventeenth century which eventually destroyed the Orthodox Tsardom'.

After the fall of Constantinople to the Turks in 1453 and the victories of Ivan the Terrible over the Tatar Khans a century later, many Orthodox Christians in the Near East began to acclaim Moscow as 'the Third Rome'. A complex of events led to the growth of this conviction. In 1439 the leaders of the Russian Church had been dismayed by the news that at the Council of Florence the representatives of the hard-pressed Byzantine Emperor and the Patriarch of Constantinople had, as the Russians thought, betrayed the cause of Eastern Orthodoxy and surrendered their birthright to Roman Catholicism. In this perspective the fall of Constantinople was regarded as an act of divine retribution on the apostate Greeks. So when Ivan the Third married Sophia Paleologos, the niece of the last Byzantine Emperor, adopted the two-headed Byzantine eagle as his heraldic symbol, and proclaimed himself 'Tsar' – that is 'Emperor' – some Orthodox thought that God had selected him to take over from Constantinople the task of leading and protecting the Orthodox everywhere.

At that time many Russians themselves saw their recovery of power and glory after centuries of suffering and humiliation as a kind of resurrection symbolized by the phoenix. They felt that they had been entrusted with responsibility for safeguarding the true faith. A Russian monk named Philotheos wrote: 'The Church of Rome fell through its heresy. The second Rome, which is Constantinople, fell to the infidel Turks. Moscow, the Third Rome, stands fast. A fourth there cannot be!' So the ideas and ideals of the 'possessors' were being put into practice. The Tsar himself was accorded quasi-ecclesiastical dignity. As a kind of priest-king he was expected to observe a rule of attendances at daily services more appropriate for a monastery than a court. The chief aim of the Tsardom was described as 'the salvation of the people'.

But the reality was very far indeed from the ideal. After the death of his first wife Anastasia Romanova, Ivan became prey to fears and suspicions somewhat similar to those which afflicted Stalin in our own time. He married one wife after another, provoked the enmity of the boyars by his outrageous cruelty and debauchery, reduced the finances of the country to ruin, ordered the Metropolitan of Moscow to be strangled because he had dared to rebuke his immorality, and killed his eldest son in a fit of rage. So his long reign of forty years ended in tragedy.

His devout but somewhat feeble-minded son Theodore had a short but peaceful reign notable only for the recognition of the Metropolitan of Moscow as a Patriarch by the Patriarchs of Constantinople and the other Eastern Orthodox Churches. When Theodore died without an heir, the House of Rurik, which had ruled for seven hundred years, came to an end.

After his death the Russian state began to slide down into anarchy, partly as the result of a series of bad harvests which drove the peasants to desperation. Opera-goers in the West may have some inkling of the tragic fate of the next Tsar, Boris Godunov, but the details of what is remembered in Russian history as 'the time of the troubles' (1598 to 1613) need not detain us. It is sufficient to note that the unbridled pursuit of private and class interests, giving rise to numerous acts of treachery and deceit, led to a state of chaos which benefited only Russia's Polish and Swedish enemies. The boyars attacked the government they were supposed to serve; serfs rebelled against the landowners; Cossacks robbed and devastated large areas in the south, and one faction actually invited a Polish force to occupy the Moscow Kremlin.

In Peter Ustinov's words, 'so excessive were the demonstrations of cupidity, so charged the outbursts of hatred, and so utterly crazed the ambition, superstition and absurdity of the principal players, that even Shakespeare would have found it impossible to invest the shower of occurrences with either logic or motivation.' One 'false Dmitri', claiming to be Ivan's eldest son, seized power for a year and then lost it. Just when another pretender looked like gaining sufficient support to restore order he was murdered by a Tatar. When armies raised by the Cossacks and the landowners came together to drive the Poles out of the Kremlin, the leader of the landowners was murdered by a Cossack. Even the church leaders were for a time too involved in the factional fighting.

But at last the nightmare came to an end. Although he was a prisoner of the Poles, who later starved him to death, Yermogen, the 76-year-old head of the Church, succeeded in despatching appeals to all the provinces to rally to the national cause. The great fortified monastery of St Sergius and the Holy Trinity added greatly to the prestige of the Church by withstanding the attacks of a Polish army for sixteen months. At last a national Russian army compelled the Polish garrison of the Kremlin to surrender. And in 1613 the leaders of the army, the boyars, the landowners and the Cossacks assembled in Moscow in a popular Parliament or 'Zemsky Sobor' for the election of a new Tsar. The choice fell on Michael Romanov who was descended from the family of Anastasia Romanova, Ivan's first wife. His father, Filaret, became Patriarch in 1619. (He had become a bishop after his wife had entered a convent.)

For the next few years father and son, Patriarch and Tsar, ruling their respective realms in harmonious fulfilment of the Byzantine ideal, were able to restore and hold the various factions together again. While the Turkish armies were overrunning south-east Europe and even reached the walls of Vienna, Russian forces were at last able to subdue the last Tatar strongholds on the Volga. Cossacks began their spectacular explorations and settlement of Siberia, and Moscow began to fulfil its destiny as 'the Third Rome' to which suppliants from the oppressed Orthodox populations of the Near East came for help.

Michael Romanov reigned from 1613 to 1645. His father, the Patriarch Filaret, was a prelate of outstanding ability who even made his mark on western European politics. With the encouragement of Cardinal Richelieu he persuaded the Poles to make peace with the Swedes and so enabled the Swedish King Gustavus Adolphus to break the power of the Habsburg armies. The Swedes showed their gratitude by sending military experts to Moscow to train a new Russian army. At the same time foreign trade with England, Germany and Holland increased greatly. Large numbers of European merchants came to live in a suburb of Moscow; but characteristically, severe measures were taken to isolate them and to prevent religious and other cultural contacts with Russian people.

Michael's successor, Tsar Alexis, also had a long and prosperous reign (1645–76). He was a pious and courageous soldier who successfully strengthened the link between the Ukraine and Moscow. However, military and commercial expansion led to increased exploitation of the peasantry both by lay landowners and by the Church which still owned enormous estates. Successive imperial decrees, including one which forbade the peasants to leave their villages, eventually reduced the majority of the peasants to the status of serfs. This impoverishment of the villagers was later to lead to desperate peasant risings, but for the time being the Byzantine alliance of Church and state, Tsar and Patriarch, favoured by the Josephian party in the Church continued to work well for both parties. Russia became a land of services and fasts universally observed by Tsar, nobility and peasants.

But Nicolas Zernov observes that 'behind this brilliant façade there were other facts which contradicted these appearances. The long services were little understood by the people. Russia's great piety and love of ritual went side by side with superstition, ignorance and immorality. There was much cruelty and corruption. Learning was almost non-existent, and most of the clergy had only the book knowledge necessary to enable them to recite the daily services. Even among the bishops there was little education, and ignorance of the simplest facts of the Christian religion was common.' In Zernov's view the victory of the Josephians had been achieved at the cost of the loss of spiritual liberty. 'The Russian Church ceased to think, its growth was stopped, its moral influence shaken, and it became a helpless victim of the arbitrary will of the Tsars ... The great vision of Russia's universal mission became the source of an extreme national pride, which isolated the country from the rest of the world.'

But in 1652 a most remarkable man was elected Patriarch of Moscow at the exceptionally early age of forty-two. Dean Stanley in his famous nineteenth-century lectures on the Eastern Church described him as 'unquestionably the greatest character in the history of the Russian hierarchy', and Nicolas Zernov says that he changed the whole course of Russian church history and compares him with Peter the Great, who, he wrote, 'strikingly resembled him both in his gifts and in his limitations'. His name was Nikon. His English contemporary Archbishop Laud shared his reforming zeal and willingness to use the power of the state to enforce liturgical changes and more orderly worship, but Laud was a far less important figure in church history.

Although Nikon exercised supreme power in the Church for only six years he set in motion an extraordinary variety of reforms. With princely munificence he founded hospitals and almshouses for orphans, widows and old people. By inviting the Tsar's wife to attend church services publicly he manifested his desire to liberate Russian women from restrictions derived from Islam. He made determined efforts to cure the habitual drunkenness of so many of the clergy. He restarted the printing presses and the programme of education introduced in the early years of Ivan the Terrible a century earlier. He astonished his contemporaries by regularly preaching on the epistle or gospel sung in the Liturgy.

He made a vital contribution to the development of Russian liturgical music by replacing the cruder musical tradition of Moscow by the more melodious tones developed in the Ukraine. He sent scholars to Greek monasteries to collate manuscripts of the Bible so that more accurate translations into Slavonic could be made. He dared to go some way towards recognizing the validity of Roman Catholic baptisms. But his attempt to conform the corrupt texts of the Slavonic liturgy to the Greek originals had disastrous results for himself and for the unity of the Church.

Nikon's liturgical reforms aroused deeply felt opposition for two reasons. First, as we know from protests over the introduction of the Alternative Service Book in the Church of England, many church members are very strongly attached to traditional texts and rituals. Seventeenth century Russians were even more emotionally conservative in such matters. Secondly, Nikon aroused patriotic hostility because many of the changes proposed brought the Slavonic texts and Russian liturgical customs into line with the practices of the Greek Churches. Those who were proud to think of Moscow as 'the Third Rome' did not see why they should conform to the uses of the Constantinople which had been in captivity to the Turks for two hundred years, and which, in Russian eyes, had betrayed the faith in 1439.

The most conspicuous of the changes which Nikon tried to enforce was the use of three fingers instead of two in making the sign of the cross. In the nineteenth century Dean Stanley observed that modern Western Christians, astonished by the passions aroused over such 'infinitely insignificant' matters, should reflect on the violence of English 'parties and mobs which had been formed to attack or defend a surplice, to reform or oppose a rubric'. Such apparently minor matters had great symbolic importance for many worshippers. Archpriest Avvakum, an exceptionally gifted priest who was in favour of many of Nikon's other attempts to renovate the Church, wrote that when the instruction came through that the sign of the cross should be made with three fingers 'according to the tradition of the holy Apostles and the Fathers', 'it was as if winter had come. Our hearts froze, our limbs shook, and a voice came from the icons:

"The hour of tribulation has come. It behoves you to suffer and be strong."'

The Patriarch did not hesitate to use force to intimidate those who refused to alter the books, rites and ceremonies to which they had been accustomed. His severity exasperated the clergy, while his arrogance enraged the nobles, but for several years his position was reasonably secure because he enjoyed the warm friendship and support of the Tsar. Indeed the story goes that he had at first refused the offer of the Patriarchate until the Tsar, nobles and bishops, prostrating themselves to the ground had solemnly promised 'to keep the commandments of Christ's holy Gospels and the canons of the holy Apostles and Fathers, and to obey the Patriarch as their chief pastor and supreme father'.

Church Councils in 1654, 1655 and 1656 supported Nikon, and he naturally had the approval of his Greek fellow-patriarchs; but the indignation aroused by his harsh treatment of his opponents increased the strength of the opposition. In these circumstances it was essential to retain the support of the Tsar, but Nikon rashly and insensitively chose this moment to attempt to redefine the relationship. In the absence of the Tsar he was accustomed to undertake many imperial responsibilities and he also had a theoretically justified desire to assert the constitutional independence of the Church on papal lines. But the way in which he set about attaining his objectives bitterly offended the nobility and began to exasperate the Tsar. The end came abruptly as a result of his own misreading of the situation. In 1658, after six years of intense activity, he became aware of the growing strength of the opposition. Accordingly he announced his resignation in the expectation that the Tsar and bishops would entreat him to resume his position as Patriarch with renewed authority. In the event he was deposed and had to retire to a monastery. One result of his miscalculation was that the Tsar and the nobles began to realize the vulnerability of the imposing structure of the Church. The schism of the Old Believers which followed still further weakened ecclesiastical resistance to aggression by the state, and the results were seen forty years later when Peter the Great made the Church a buttress of the imperial regime.

4
'Orthodoxy, Autocracy, Patriotism'

During the two hundred years from 1700 to 1900 the story of the Russian Church is full of contradictions. On one side it is seen as an instrument of Tsarist despotism and reaction. On the other side there are evidences of brilliant spiritual life bursting up through the limitations imposed upon it. In this chapter we set positive and negative elements in the picture side by side.

Peter the Great (1682–1725) was a man of gigantic stature physically, mentally and in the strength of his will. He is one of the very few rulers who actually reorientated the outlook and history of his country. His aim was to transform a backward medieval state and society into a secular power comparable to the kingdoms of contemporary western Europe. Inevitably he utterly rejected the idea of Moscow as 'the Third Rome'. As a Western-style rationalist he regarded the Church as a major obstacle to modernization. So he 'beheaded' it, first by refusing to allow the election of a patriarch, and then, after it had been leaderless for twenty years, abolishing the patriarchate altogether and replacing it with a committee called 'The Holy Synod'.

The Holy Synod was modelled on the constitutions of some Lutheran Churches in Germany. It did indeed consist predominantly of bishops, but the real power was exercised by the Ober-procurator, a lay official appointed by the Emperor. He set the agenda and dictated the decisions. As in England after the Reformation all the bishops were appointed by the sovereign, but in Russia state control became even more extensive. Lay representatives of the Emperor were appointed to supervise the work of every diocese. As the years went by it became the custom to move the bishops from one diocese to another with increasing frequency, thus reducing their influence on their flocks. (By 1914, many bishops were only allowed to serve two or three years in a diocese before being moved on.) Peter's successors followed Henry the Eighth's example by seizing the Church's landed estates and distributing them to their faithful followers. Thus the higher clergy became dependent on state subsidies, and the parochial clergy on the fees they could exact from their parishioners. The Church was deprived of any vestige of financial independence. At the same time the westernized, secular society of the new capital of St Petersburg was so hostile to the old Orthodox tradition that the Church lost almost all real influence on the social and political actions of the ruling classes. Even though a Christian veneer remained, their prophet was the sceptical French philosopher Voltaire rather than St Sergius. For two hundred years the Church was used as a buttress for the imperial regime. This conjunction was summed up in the nineteenth-century slogan, 'Orthodoxy, Autocracy, Patriotism'.

On the surface the Church appeared to benefit from this relationship. Many magnificent cathedrals, monasteries and parish churches were built. The principal bishops were enabled to live in grand style. Imperial ceremonies such as coronations were celebrated by the Church with great splendour. The clergy were authorized to act as registrars of births, marriages and deaths. Missionary activities among the pagan tribes of Siberia and the Muslims of Central Asia were facilitated by the government. In the nineteenth century financial support from the state enabled church schools to be opened in towns and villages all over the country. Police powers were available to harass or suppress 'rival' congregations of Old Believers and Protestants. It was an offence to try to convert a Russian to another 'faith' (see Chapter 6 below).

But the Church had to pay a heavy price for these ambiguous benefits. Its leaders were expected to give unstinted support to the regime. Parish priests were expected to act as informers for the police. The Church was administered in a rigidly conservative spirit. Partly as a result of the seizure of monastic lands during the reign of Catherine II (1762–96), over seven hundred of the 954 monasteries were closed for long periods. While some of the bishops enjoyed life at the court, the village priests and their impoverished parishioners viewed St Petersburg with deep suspicion. Only the assiduously nurtured cult of the Emperor as the 'Little Father' of his people remained as a bridge between the court and the peasants.

But the superstitiousness of the peasants was as notorious as their loyalty (at this time) to their image of the Tsar. Professor Leo Zander of the Russian Orthodox Theological Academy in Paris once told me of a comical incident that occurred as late as 1915. He was then serving as librarian to the Imperial General Staff. As a staff officer he was expected to wear a sword, but being a very small man he found it more convenient to equip himself with a light wooden replica supplied by a theatrical agency. Unfortunately during a parade in heavy rain, as he rode past the troops, his sword slipped from his belt, fell into a pool of water and *floated*. The peasants hailed this as a miracle and were with difficulty quietened down.

Happily there were many signs of real spiritual life in the Church despite its exploitation by the Tsarist state. Theological academies were established in Moscow and St Petersburg, which produced works of serious scholarship. Great bishops, such as Filaret Drozdov (1782–1867), Metropolitan of Moscow in the nineteenth century, were acclaimed internationally for their learning and eloquence as preachers. His spirituality was expressed in prayers like this:

> Lord, I know not what to ask of thee. Thou alone knowest what are my true needs. Thou lovest me more than I myself know how to love. Help me to see my real needs. I dare not ask either a cross or consolation. I can only wait on thee. My heart is open to thee. Visit and help me for thy great mercy's sake. Strike me and heal me, cast me down and raise me up. I worship in silence thy holy will and thy inscrutable ways. I offer myself as a sacrifice to thee. I have no other desire than to fulfil thy will. Teach me how to pray. Pray thou thyself in me.

A powerful movement for spiritual renewal had begun in some of the monasteries in the eighteenth century. For example St Demetrius of Rostov, a contemporary of Peter the Great, wrote meditations on the Holy Liturgy of which this is a brief extract:

Come, O my Light, and lighten my darkness! Come, O my Life, and quicken my deadness! Come, O my Healer, and heal my wounds! Come, O Fire divine, scorch the thorns of my sins and set my heart ablaze with the fire of thy Love! Come, O my King, sit on the throne of my heart and rule over it! For thou alone art my King and my Lord!

He was one of the harbingers of a succession of holy monks and spiritual directors known as *Startsi* or 'Elders', who left their mark in nineteenth-century Russian literature. For example, in *The Brothers Karamazov* Dostoevsky contrasts the *starets* Zossima with Ivan, who represents the mentality of the godless intelligentsia. Indeed Ivan's famous parable of the Grand Inquisitor powerfully evokes the conflict between the 'possessors' and the 'non-possessors' four hundred years earlier (see page 15), and between bishops who were dutiful servants of the state and their critics in the nineteenth century. It is still relevant to reflection on the situation of the Moscow Patriarchate in the Soviet state today.

The most famous centre of the revived tradition of the 'non-possessors' was the monastery of Optina Pustyn in the Kaluga forest south of Moscow. A long succession of Elders there had been inspired by the Russian monk Paisi Velichkovski (1722–94), abbot of the monastery of Niamets in Moldavia. He translated into Slavonic the *Philokalia* – a classical collection of extracts from the Greek Fathers on self-examination, prayer and mystical communion with God. As the ministry of the Elders of Optina became more widely known, pilgrims began to come from all over European Russia seeking spiritual help. (There is a parallel with the extraordinary attraction of the Curé d'Ars in France at the same period.) Not all the Elders were priests. Some were simple hermits. Their advice was often sought on worldly as well as religious matters. Often they were asked to lay hands on the sick or to pray for their healing. Often too they manifested extraordinary powers of insight or clairvoyance.

Dostoevsky wrote a vivid description of a typical Elder:

Zossima was sixty-five. He came of a family of landowners, had been in the army and served in the Caucasus as an officer. Afterwards he became a monk and after some years so many people came to him for confession, advice and healing that he had acquired the keenest intuition and could tell from an unknown face what the newcomer wanted. He was not at all stern. On the contrary he was almost cheerful. The monks said that he was more drawn to those who were more sinful, and the greater the sinner the more he loved him. Pilgrims of the humbler class came from all over Russia to see him and obtain his blessing. They fell down before him, kissed his feet and brought him the sick 'possessed of devils'. The Elder spoke to them, read a brief prayer over them and dismissed them. For the humble soul of the Russian peasant, worn out by grief and toil and still more by everlasting injustice and sin, his own and the world's, it was the greatest comfort to find someone holy to fall down before and worship.

(*The Brothers Karamazov*, part 1, book 1, chapter 5).

Three actual exponents of this powerful mystical tradition may be mentioned. One was St Tikhon of Zadonsk (1724–83). The son of an impoverished church reader, he rose rapidly through the ecclesiastical schools to become rector of the seminary at Novgorod. He read many Protestant and Roman Catholic books in Latin, and actually translated into Russian a book of 'Spiritual Treasures' compiled by a seventeenth-century Anglican Bishop of Norwich. He was consecrated bishop and put in charge of the diocese of Voronezh. But after four years he resigned and retired to the small monastery of Zadonsk, where he meditated continually on the 'double-eternity' of death and the vision of the heavenly world. He constantly read the Bible and the Fathers, and often spent all night meditating on the Psalms. He had several extraordinary visions. He regularly distributed his income to the poor, and showed great patience and humility in counselling the streams of peasants, prisoners and children who sought his guidance and blessing.

St Serafim of Sarov (1759–1833) became even better known as a teacher of the way of holiness. After seventeen years spent in complete seclusion, at the age of sixty-six he opened the door of his cell to those who sought his help, and soon hundreds of pilgrims began to come to him. Although his bent body witnessed to the severity of the ascetic discipline to which he had submitted for so long and to a beating inflicted by robbers, he always radiated joy – indeed his characteristic greeting to a penitent was 'My Joy!'. He had remarkable gifts of perception and healing, and many compared him to the spiritual Fathers and miracle-workers of the fourth-century Church. He was also hailed as the heir of St Nil Sorsky (see page 15 above). He boldly invited lay people to share more deeply in the gifts of the Spirit and in mystical prayer, and long after his death he had a profound influence on leaders of the 'Russian Spiritual Renaissance' of the early twentieth century (see page 16 below).

The third in this succession was Alexander Michaelovich Grenkov (1812–91) better known as Starets Amvrosy. In 1839, at the age of twenty-seven, he felt an overwhelming call to go to the Optina Pustyn monastery. Twenty years later, after recovering from a very severe illness, he was recognized as a leading spiritual authority, and continued to minister to the community and to innumerable visitors for the next thirty years. Dostoevsky and Tolstoy and many members of the sceptical Russian intelligentsia came to see him, and he answered letters from a large number of correspondents. Despite his poor health, he used to hear the Morning Office at four a.m., have a frugal breakfast and then dictate letters until ten. Thereafter, with only slight intermissions for food and rest, he would receive visitors and hear confessions until late in the evening. There are numerous accounts of healings through the laying on of his hands and his prayers, and he helped a great many penitents to overcome their misery and despair and to make a new start with deepened faith.

Father Amvrosy himself commended *The Way of a Pilgrim*, an anonymous work by a layman, first published in Russian in 1884 and translated into English and reprinted several times this century. It is probably the most accessible expression of Russian spirituality of the last century. It is not completely typical but it is a moving account of a spiritual pilgrimage. It could be described as a commentary on the constantly repeated 'Jesus Prayer': 'Lord Jesus Christ, Son of God, have mercy on me, a sinner'.

Pilgrims came not only from European Russia but also from the vast spaces of Siberia. Writers insufficiently aware of the extensive missionary work of the Russian Church under the Empire, too often condemn Orthodoxy for a lack of missionary zeal. But under the inspiration of great missionary pioneers, such as Bishop Innocenti of Kamchatka (1797–1879), Orthodox mission Churches were founded in Japan, and Orthodox missionaries travelled to Alaska and down the Pacific coast of North America as far as San Francisco.

The Russian Church has also been falsely accused of lack of social concern. But many Christian individuals and groups strove to alleviate the desperate lot of poor people in the great cities, and some very active movements for social reform were led by some devout aristocrats. For example, the Grand Duchess Elizabeth (whose husband was assassinated by terrorists in 1905) founded in Moscow a 'Martha-Mary House of Mercy' for deaconesses, who combined a contemplative life with devoted work for the poor. They ran a hospital under the guidance of the best doctors, a home for abandoned children, a reformatory for prostitutes, and an invalid home for soldiers and sailors wounded in the Russo-Japanese war. They also visited in the slums, nursing the sick, cleaning up, supplying and cooking food and caring for babies as well as offering spiritual ministrations.

But once again we need to recall the contradictions in the life of the pre-revolutionary Church. On the one hand there were many evidences of spiritual vitality. On the other the official leadership of the Church was being effectively subordinated to the perpetuation of the Tsarist autocracy. This control was, as we have noted, exercised principally through the office of the Ober-procurator of the Holy Synod. And often the holders of that office were by no means unChristian or evil men.

The best known of them was Konstantin Pobedonostev, who has often been represented as the evil genius of the Russian Church at the turn of the century. He certainly was very conservatively minded and ruled the Church with a rod of iron, but it is equally clear from the records that he was a sincerely convinced and extremely intelligent Christian. He was a friend of Dostoevsky and is said to have influenced the writing of the parable of the Grand Inquisitor. It is interesting to compare his contemporary with his posthumous reputation. For example, when the learned and far-sighted Anglican Bishop Mandell Creighton visited Moscow to represent the Archbishop of Canterbury at the coronation of Nicholas II in 1896, he described Pobedonostev as 'one of the most able and interesting men he had ever met'. In conversation with the English bishop, the Ober-procurator justified his ultra-conservative policy on the grounds that it 'corresponded to the needs of the Russian people ... The services of the Church were pure poetry and impressed the great truths of religion on the popular mind ... You may speak of superstition in the veneration of icons, but', he said, 'that veneration was a prayer struggling for expression. It might not be possible to explain how it appealed to the ignorant mind, but nothing was free from superstition.' In his opinion, 'the superstitions of free-thinkers went deeper than anything that could be put down to the most ignorant Christian.'

Pobedonostev concluded his conversation with the English bishop with some comments on the relationship between Russian Orthodoxy and other Christian confessions. He represented a widely held view according to which 'Rome was the greatest enemy of the Russian Church'. As for Western Protestants his opinion was that 'the Bible without the Church could be made to mean anything'.

But there were other Orthodox laymen who took a less reactionary and more ecumenical attitude. Their writings are evidence that the intellectual life of the Russian Church in the nineteenth century was far from being as moribund as is often assumed. These lay theologians and Christian philosophers were able to write more freely than bishops and theologians of the state-controlled Church. One of them was Ivan Kireyevsky (b.1806), who was deeply influenced by the Elders of Optina, and who himself influenced the 'Slavophils' – those intellectuals who opposed the atheistic Western philosophies of the majority of the intelligentsia. He criticized 'Western men' as being 'under the sway of an exclusive development of abstract reasoning' and contrasted with it the creative, mystical and dynamic forms of cognition which exercise the whole of a man in all his activities.

Eastern Orthodox thinkers in their search for truth should be concerned with the right disposition, with the inner wholeness of the thinking man, whereas typical Western thinkers were too exclusively concerned with the interrelation of abstract ideas. The knowledge of God was not given to individuals in isolation but it was mediated through the community of the Church.

A. S. Khomyakov (1804–60) was much better known outside Russia. He also taught the entireness, the inner 'totality' of man as necessary for the apprehension of divine truth, and stressed the role of the church as the Body of Christ, uniting, transforming and illuminating the spirit of man by the Spirit of God. 'No one is saved alone: he who is saved is saved in the Church as its member along with other members. If one believes, it is as a member of the community of love. If any one prays, he is in the community of prayer. It is the Spirit of Love who prays in you.' Khomyakov combined his strenuous work as a Christian philosopher with intensive efforts to improve the conditions of life of the peasants. (In his time serfdom had not yet been abolished.)

The third notable Christian writer of this period was Vladimir Soloviev (1853–1900). He was more at home in St Petersburg than the other two. He wrote in the style of contemporary Western philosophy but caused a sensation in intellectual circles by going to attend lectures at the Theological Academy. The incarnation of the Son of God was central to his thought and he looked for the sanctification of the whole created order. His favourite concept was the 'God-manhood', the transfiguration or 'divinization' of human nature and the created world. Some detected a dangerous pantheistic tendency in his earlier works, but in later life he strongly expressed his ardent faith in Christ as Lord and Victor. His ideas were strongly denounced by Pobedonostev as Utopian, and his concept of the reconciliation of the Eastern Churches with Rome was far in advance of his time, as was his teaching that nationalism destroys a nation. But he was a notable forerunner of the Ecumenical Movement of the later twentieth century.

But is it possible to build up a more inclusive picture of the life of the Russian Church at the turn of the century outside the two capitals? Behind the glittering façade of St Petersburg with its Western European orientation, and the romantic ideas of 'the People' entertained by the Slavophils of Moscow, the general state of the Church in the country did not appear to be very promising despite the widespread influence of some outstanding Elders. Few foreign visitors, who were sumptuously entertained in St Petersburg or Moscow, were able to visit the villages in which the majority of the population lived in ignorance and poverty. In 1914 a pious Balliol scholar, whom I knew later, was engaged as a tutor by a princely family. In their splendid palace in St Petersburg they all spoke French and behaved like highly cultivated Europeans. But when they went down to their huge rural estate for the summer, the atmosphere changed completely. For example, when the steward had been ordered to beat the sons of the house for disobeying their tutor, the two boys took whips and went through the village beating every peasant they could find.

The parish priests in such villages were only a little better educated than most of the other peasants. They lived by taking fees in kind for administering the sacraments and blessing houses and crops and other objects and by cultivating their own gardens or smallholdings. A book published in English in 1970 contains a graphic description of a village priest written a hundred years earlier by the half-English daughter of a wealthy landowner. She wrote: 'The village folk disliked and feared the priest. My father was slightly contemptuous of him. Enormously fat, of middle height, his red beard always raddled, his tangled hair falling down his neck, Father Vassily would have made a king of beggars. He would beg, steal or take the last hen from a widow for her husband's funeral. Father Vassily did not scruple to demand a sack of potatoes for a brief visit to a sick parishioner. He had a plot of land attached to his little house, but he and his fat wife were too lazy to look after a cow or a sow, or to sow a row of beans.' Distressing reports of this kind have to be set alongside the idealized pictures of the peasantry painted by the Slavophil or Populist students who were being urged 'to go to the People'.

Doubtless there were many devout and pastorally minded priests, but they have left little trace in Russian literature available in English. Nicolas Zernov writes of the conditions in which even the most committed village priest had to work under the old regime: 'The chief defect of the clergy was their lack of authority. They were helpless against the petty officials who filled the diocesan offices, and who were responsible to no one but the lay Procurator. They were also at the mercy of the local police, looked down upon by the intelligentsia, and not much respected by the peasants on whose liberality they depended for their very existence.'

It may of course be argued that the poor education and lack of pastoral concern of many of the country clergy had much less serious effects on the life of Russian parishes than similar deficiencies would have in Protestant Churches in Western Europe. The spirituality of the vast mass of the Russian peasants was moulded unconsciously by custom and attendance at the Liturgy. Teaching, preaching and example were less essential. It did not matter so much that a priest was ignorant, drunken and coarse, so long as he still remembered how he had been taught to celebrate the Liturgy. Customs such as severe fasting in Lent and at other seasons were still widely observed even by infrequent churchgoers. Most houses had an icon corner where traditional prayers were sometimes said. Large numbers of older people made pilgrimages on foot to distant holy places or holy men. Many could be deeply stirred by the drama of the Liturgy, particularly at major festivals. Some had a simple personal prayer life. Others devoted themselves to works of charity. It is impossible for an outsider to assess the significance of such considerations.

In the major towns the clergy were better educated. Many fine churches were built, served by devoted priests and furnished with rich vestments and excellent choirs. But there was little effective religious education for the young. The intellectual atmosphere of the high schools and universities continued to be strongly anti-religious. The Church had no synodical organs for self-government, and almost no independence from the Tsarist state either nationally or locally. The bishops were all appointed by the Tsar acting through the Holy Synod controlled by the Ober-procurator in the interest of the autocracy. All church publications were rigorously censored. In theory every sermon had to be submitted in writing to the state authorities before delivery. (This meant that many priests never preached at all.) Some bishops and professors of theology were excellent academic theologians and eloquent preachers; some were skilful politicians; some were devout men with little interest in political or social questions.

The bishops had few opportunities to confer together or to consult one another. Many of the best simply concentrated on their own diocese – though even then they were liable to be moved on in an arbitrary way if the government considered that they showed too much zeal or independence. Moreover the exceptionally great difficulties of travel in rural Russia in many months of the year prevented the bishops from having close or frequent contacts with outlying parishes. In general it must be said that Russian bishops had nothing like the authority in ecclesiastical and local affairs exercised until very recently by the metropolitans of small dioceses in Greece.

The contrasts and contradictions noted in this chapter show the very great difficulty of reaching an accurate picture of the life of the Russian Church before the Revolution. But we may conclude with some relevant statistics. Before 1914 the Church was served by 163 bishops in 73 dioceses assisted by 51,105 parish clergy ministering in 54,174 church buildings. There were over 1000 monasteries and convents, 94,629 monks and nuns, 4 Theological Academies, 57 seminaries and 185 'pre-theological schools' (chiefly for sons of the clergy irrespective of whether they had any vocation to the priesthood – Stalin was a student at a seminary in Georgia). The Church also directed 37,528 government-financed parochial schools and managed 34,497 parish libraries.

But how would this apparently imposing institution stand up to the shock of a Communist Revolution? Before we try to answer that question we must consider some remarkable evidences of spiritual renewal which surfaced in the first years of this century.

5
Signs of Renewal

The Russian Orthodox Church before the Bolshevik revolution is generally believed to have been a moribund and ultra-conservative institution unduly subservient to the Tsarist state. This was the view taken for granted by the Russian intelligentsia before 1917 and propagated by pro-communist publicists ever since. But from the beginning of this century there were at least three lively signs of renewal within the Church. One was the demand for freedom from state control. One was involvement in movements for political and social reform; and the third was the call for a profound philosophical and theological revolution.

The most substantial evidence for the existence of these more positive elements in the pre-revolutionary Church is to be found in the too often forgotten developments between the abdication of the Tsar in March 1917 and the communist takeover in October of the same year. This was indeed the only period during the last two hundred and eighty years when the Russian Church was free to begin to be its true self. Before March 1917 it was subjected to Tsarist oppression. After October 1917 it was the victim of communist propaganda and persecution. Unfortunately the movements for the reform of the Church, which came into the open during this brief period of freedom, are almost unknown to most Christians outside Russia.

Despite the apparent stability and ubiquity of the Orthodox Church at the beginning of the century, many far-sighted clerics and laymen had become aware of the need for reform. Some church leaders had come to the conclusion that the 'Ecclesiastical Regulation' imposed by Peter the Great in 1721 was contrary to the canon law of the Church. Others questioned the long continued repression of the Old Believers and Protestant nonconformists by both state and Church. For example, Metropolitan Anthony Vadkovsky of

St Petersburg (1846–1912) took the lead in working for change. He was deeply concerned about the alienation of the Russian intelligentsia from the Church, which they despised and dismissed as being merely an arm of the Tsarist state. The Metropolitan encouraged students at the Theological Academy to study the moral and sociological ideologies of the secular world. He promoted meetings between theologians and artists – including Sergei Diaghilev, the world-famous promoter of the Russian ballet. And with his blessing, a 'Religious Philosophical Society' was formed in 1901 to discuss such questions as religious freedom and the place of women in Russian society. (The Society was suppressed by the police after two years!)

The defeat of the Russian forces by the Japanese in 1904–5 gave a fresh impetus to movements for reform both in politics and in the Orthodox Church. The Ober-procurator, Konstantin Pobedonostev, was becoming old and ill and losing his grip on the Holy Synod. Metropolitan Anthony persuaded the Tsar and his Council of Ministers to ease restrictions on the Old Believers and Protestants on the grounds that 'repression of non-Orthodox minorities exacerbated civil violence'. And he warned the government that toleration for the minorities must soon be followed by the restoration of canonical freedom to the Orthodox Church.

At the same time a movement for social reform came up from lower levels in the Church. Its best known leader was Fr Georgii Gapon (1870–1906), a priest from the Ukraine educated at the St Petersburg Academy, who had been deeply influenced by Tolstoy. He was scandalized by the wealth of some of the monasteries. He repudiated Peter the Great's assumption that it was the duty of priests to report to the police any evidence of sedition that came to them through hearing confessions. He believed that the Tsarist regime could only be preserved if it made moderate 'liberal' reforms. And in 1904 he became actively engaged in the inauguration of the 'Association of Factory and Plant Workers' – an elementary form of trade union.

Fr Gapon tried to persuade the Prime Minister (Witte), Maxim Gorki and other influential people to protect the new Association against the factory owners' determined attempts to destroy it. In January 1905 the work-force at the great Putilov heavy industrial works in St Petersburg went on strike. They demanded better working conditions, the setting up of an arbitration board and increased civil rights. When the management refused to consider these demands, Fr Gapon organized a traditional 'procession of the cross' to petition the Tsar to recognize the rights of industrial workers. But his hopes of a peaceful ending of the conflict ended in tragedy. When, on what came to be called 'Bloody Sunday', processions of thousands of unarmed workers carrying icons and portraits of the Tsar approached the Winter Palace, the troops stationed in the surrounding streets panicked and opened fire. At least two hundred people were killed and hundreds more were wounded. Fr Gapon himself went into exile and was later assassinated.

Meanwhile some of the bishops were pressing the case for Church reform. Pobedonostev persuaded the Emperor to refer the question from the Council of Ministers to the Holy Synod which he normally controlled. But he was unable to be present at the crucial meeting, and the bishops took the opportunity to petition the Tsar to allow a representative Church Council to be called, which would consider reforms including the restoration of the patriarchate. The Emperor agreed in principle that a council should meet but postponed fixing a date for convening it. The announcement nevertheless provoked intensive debates in the press and in church circles. For example, thirty-two priests published a statement that the Church must at last be cleared of the charge of suppressing religious freedom. This had been done by the state in the name of the Church and under the pretence of defending her; but it had been done against her will and against her spirit. They demanded 'a return to the ancient canonical order based on self-government and independence from the state.' Commissions of bishops compiled substantial reports for consideration by the Council; but, advised by a more conservative prime minister, the Tsar still gave no indication of a date for it.

Then in 1909 seven prominent writers shocked readers by publishing an all-out attack on the atheism and 'irresponsible anarchism' of the Russian intelligentsia. The writers of

Fr Sergei Bulgakov

this collection of essays entitled *Vekhi* (*Signposts*) were former Marxists of high academic standing. They denounced the secular utopianism of the left and asserted the necessity of a religious foundation for a consistent philosophy of life. They repudiated terrorism as a 'bet on an historical gamble' and as provoking popular unrest to a point at which all regular government and properly planned reforms would become impossible. So wrote Peter Struve, a leading economist. Nicholas Berdyaev, a philosopher who had suffered some years of exile for criticizing the subjection of the Holy Synod to the autocracy, attacked the immorality of the revolutionary parties. He wrote that 'the misfortune of the Russian intelligentsia is that its love for justice and for the welfare of the common people has paralysed and almost killed its love for truth'.

Sergei Bulgakov (one of the most impressive personalities I have ever met), who had been professor of Political Economy at Kiev, and who was later elected as a member of the second Duma (the parliamentary body set up after 1905), drew attention to the 'strange ways in whch the ardent orations of the atheistic left' echoed 'the Orthodox outlook'. They called for 'social repentance not before God but before the peasants and the proletariat: willingness to sacrifice combined with dogmatic and credulous atheism.' The intelligentsia, he wrote, 'vacillates between a sense of spiritual, aristocratic superiority, and worship of the common people. Both these attitudes are false.'

Most of the authors of *Signposts* continued to teach in the USSR until they were driven to emigrate in 1922 on account of their religious convictions. They became widely known and appreciated in the West in the years before the Second World War. Some English church leaders and members of the Student Christian Movement had the privilege of meeting them at conferences of the Fellowship of St Alban and St Sergius.

The outbreak of war in 1914 ended hopes for the calling of a Church Council for a time, but very shortly after the Tsar abdicated in March 1917 church leaders obtained from the Provisional Government the promise of facilities for convening it. There had been a long debate between those who thought that the Council (Sobor) should be composed only of bishops, and those who looked for a more broadly representative body; but in April 1917 a reconstituted Holy Synod announced that a Council including the bishops and representatives of the clergy and laity of each diocese would meet in Moscow in August. In July Prime Minister Kerensky appointed Professor A. V. Kartashev as Ober-procurator with a mandate to abolish his office after completing the arrangements for the Council. On 5 August the Church formally achieved its independence from state control, and on 15 August the first free Church Council to meet for over two hundred years assembled in the Uspensky Cathedral in the Kremlin.

The Council consisted of eighty bishops, one hundred and forty-nine priests, twenty-four deacons and cantors, and two hundred and ninety-nine lay representatives from the sixty-five dioceses. Thus despite all the difficulties of the political and military situation in Russia in 1917, the supposedly moribund Russian Orthodox Church was able to convene a fully representative Church Council fifty-three years before the Church of England inaugurated its General Synod. In the Russian Sobor all members had one vote, but if seventy-five per cent of the bishops refused to confirm a measure passed by the majority of the whole Council, it had to be referred back for further consideration.

The Council had before it an extensive programme of proposals for reform, but time was rapidly running out. On 26 October when the Kremlin was already being shelled by the Bolshevik forces, the Council voted to restore the patriarchate to give a lead to the Church in the troubled times ahead. As the Bolsheviks had already occupied the Kremlin the actual choice of Patriarch had to be made in the Cathedral of St Saviour where ordinary sessions of the Council were held. (The cathedral was subsequently blown up by the Soviets and later replaced by a large open-air swimming pool.) Following New Testament precedents, lots were cast after prayer for the three candidates who had received the most votes. Metropolitan Tikhon (Belyavin), born in 1865, bishop of the Russian Orthodox Church in America and chairman of the Council, became Patriarch. Permission was given for him to be enthroned in the Uspensky Cathedral in the Kremlin on 21 November 1917. This is said to be the last Christian service to have been held in this historic building.

The Council continued to meet intermittently until it was dissolved in September 1918. Its agenda gave some indications of how an independent and free Orthodox Church might have developed. But in practice it was able to achieve very little because Lenin and the Supreme Soviet gave very high priority to removing all the privileges and resources of the Church. On 4 December the first of a long series of decrees was passed, which deprived the Church of its property, of its schools, of its theological seminaries, of its hospitals and other social institutions, and of its status as a corporate legal entity. Civil rights and ration cards were removed from the clergy, and their children were debarred from higher education. All monasteries and convents were eventually closed. The Church was forbidden to publish or preach the gospel outside church buildings or to give organized religious instruction to boys and girls under eighteen.

The consequences of these decrees, and of the executions and imprisonments of bishops and priests which accompanied them, will be considered in the second part of this book. But the fact that the Church convened the Council at the earliest possible moment after it was free to do so, together with the significant programme of reforms it planned to undertake, are weighty evidence of the great potential spiritual vitality of the Russian Church as it emerged from its long years of bondage under the empire of the Tsars.

6
Nonconformists in Pre-revolutionary Russia

In England in 1632 a minister named John Lathrop was arrested at Islington near London. He and members of his congregation were brought before the courts charged with 'dishonouring God and disobeying the king by running into the woods for worship'. The Anglican authorities maintained that in the Church of England 'the pure Word of God was preached and the sacraments duly administered according to Christ's ordinance'. There was therefore no need for congregations to set up their own conventicles in private houses or in the open air. Worse still, by daring to appoint their own ministers they had broken the visible unity of the English Church. Such an action was thought to threaten the safety of the realm – for Anglicans, Presbyterians and Roman Catholics at that time fervently believed that uniformity of religious practice within a country was essential for the stability of the state. This widely held conviction (from which only Baptists and Congregationalists dissented) was one cause of the length and ferocity of the 'wars of religion' which devastated Europe in the seventeenth century. It was the principle behind Louis XIV's revocation in 1685 of the Edict of Nantes, which had given some protection to French Protestants.

If Western European rulers held so firmly for so long that Church and state must be one, it is easy to imagine how strongly Russian tsars and patriarchs were convinced of the evils of dissent and the necessity of suppressing it. The conviction that all means were justified for keeping citizens within the Orthodox fold, was reinforced by the fact that Roman Catholic Poles and Lutheran Swedes had for centuries been taking every opportunity to seize Russian territory and impose their own forms of church on the people.

(Remember the Armada!) Russian governments therefore felt justified in taking severe measures to prevent any infiltration of Catholicism or Protestantism from the West. Even though permission was given for the opening of a Lutheran church in Moscow in 1576, this was exclusively for the use of foreign traders in their ghetto, and until 1905 no Russian could legally become a member of any Church except the Orthodox. Conversely, when some foreign immigrants were later allowed to set up their own churches, their ministers were forbidden to preach in Russian.

Thus it came about that the first Russian dissenters were not proselytes or radical reformers from abroad, but ultra-conservative Orthodox believers from 'within'. How did this first schism in the seamless robe of Holy Russia come about? It resulted from the reaction of many of the faithful and some of the most devoted priests to the liturgical and other reforms introduced by Patriarch Nikon in the mid-seventeenth century (see page 22 above).

Many of Nikon's reforms seem in retrospect to have been justified on both liturgical and scholarly grounds; but they provoked deeply felt opposition among more conservatively minded believers. It would, however, be a mistake to dismiss the 'Old Believers' as mere reactionaries. Their leader Fr Avvakum (1621–82) was a most zealous and courageous priest. His autobiography, written in 1673, is still worth reading, and the fact that he wrote it in colloquial Russian rather than Slavonic, entitles him to recognition as the pioneer of modern Russian literature. He was supported during his long years of exile and missionary work in Siberia by his equally courageous wife. He was an eloquent preacher and capable organizer. He cherished the older Muscovite traditions of icon painting, and to our own time many of the finest medieval icons were preserved in 'Old Believer' churches. Conservative though he was in liturgical matters, in his sermons he was a severe critic of the greed and injustice of the wealthy and powerful. He made many enemies, and it was not surprising that he suffered excommunication by a Church Council in 1666, banishment for ten years to Siberia, and fifteen years in prison. He ended by being burnt alive as a heretic in 1682 – a hundred and twenty-seven years after Archbishop Cranmer suffered the same fate at Oxford. His spiritual influence lived on to modern times in spite of periodic outbursts of severe persecution of his followers by Church and state. In some ways he can be compared with modern martyrs of the faith in Soviet Russia who suffered imprisonment, exile and execution because they rejected the compromises which leaders of the Patriarchal and Baptist Churches made with the rulers of the Kremlin.

In the first years of their separation from the Patriarchal Church many thousands of the Old Believers were hanged or burnt alive. They were also in canonical difficulties because no bishop had gone with them into the wilderness. One minority still continues in this 'priestless' state; but the main body was later joined by a bishop who was able to assure a succession of priests. Partly because of their illegal status and the hostility of the leaders of the official Church, partly because some of them became involved in peasant revolts, and partly because of the difficulties of communication in rural Russia which prevented the formation of one consolidated ecclesiastical institution, the Old Believers divided into several different groupings, and it is almost impossible to estimate their numbers at any particular time. For example, when an official census was made in 1897, they were registered as numbering two and a quarter million, but some scholars believe that the true number was as high as fifteen million or twelve per cent of the population.

It was always difficult for Russian governments to enforce their will over the length and breadth of this vast land, so groups of Old Believers were able to survive and practise their archaic modes of life and worship even when persecution by the official Church and state was most severe. Professor Arseniev, a writer on Orthodox spirituality, described a visit to such a community before 1914. At the end of a remote forest track he met a guide who led him by an almost invisible path through a deadly swamp. Passing through another thick wood they came out on the shores of a small lake surrounded by the wooden houses of a self-supporting community of Old Believers who had preserved the speech, manners and customs of the seventeenth century.

Of course aerial surveys will now have revealed the existence of such settlements to the Soviet authorities; but it is still possible for congregations of 'unregistered' Baptists to meet secretly for worship in the forests when their places of worship have been bulldozed (see Chapter 10).

In the seventeenth century there were other small groups of more radical dissenters in remote places in south Russia. Some of these were Dukhobors who rejected the Church and much of the Bible. Many of them were transported to Transcaucasia, and later the majority emigrated to Canada where their eccentric behaviour embarrassed even a friendly democratic government. The Molokans (or 'milk-drinkers') were more numerous. Basing themselves on their own inter-pretation of the Bible, they rejected Orthodox rituals, sacra-ments and icons. They were puritanical in their morals and often won the respect of their Orthodox neighbours for their industry and reliability. But they were little known outside a few localities.

The first substantial group of Protestant dissenters were not Russians but German-speaking Mennonites, who had been driven from their homes in central Europe because they were pacifists. Catherine the Great (1762–96) settled a con-siderable colony of them on an island in the Dnieper because they had a good reputation for industry and civil order, and had practical skills in agriculture useful to the Russian economy. As they were not Russian speaking, it was held that they were not subject to the law under which all Russians had to be members of the Orthodox Church.

In the early nineteenth century Evangelical missions from Britain spread all over the world, and thus John Paterson came to Moscow in 1812 to set up a Russian Bible Society which was encouraged by Tsar Alexander I (1801–25). Five years later the London Missionary Society made contact with the Mennonites over the organization of missions to Muslims in Siberia. For some years Protestant pastors were permitted to minister to foreign congregations in St Peters-burg; but in 1841 the Holy Synod of the Orthodox Church secured a reversion to the former 'exclusive' policy and the LMS mission was suppressed.

Since 1700 the frontiers of Tsarist Russia were being

pushed ever further west, and by the middle of the nineteenth century the empire included large areas populated by
ethnic minorities of Roman Catholics, Lutherans and other
Protestants. So it came about that in 1864 the then well-
known Baptist leader Johann G. Oncken (1800–84), following contacts with Baptists in the German community at
Memel (now Klaipeda), asked the imperial government to
authorize the opening of a Baptist church in St Petersburg.
In an interview with the Minister of the Interior he affirmed
that 'if the government tries forcibly to suppress the Baptists
in Poland and Russia, they will find that it is very difficult to
destroy a genuine religious movement'. Much in the history
of Russia in the last seventy years confirms this prophecy.

In fact the earliest recorded 'baptism of believers' in
Russia took place not in St Petersburg but in Tiflis (modern
Tblisi) in 1867, where a group of Molokans came under
Baptist influence. Eight years later, when Dean Stanley of St
Paul's Cathedral was preparing to visit Moscow, Johann
Oncken asked him to intercede for Evangelicals who were
suffering persecution from the authorities in southern Russia. This Evangelical stirring seems to have had several
distinct causes. First, there were movements of spiritual
renewal among the Molokans. Secondly, German colonists
in the Ukraine stimulated among their Orthodox neighbours
a movement for a weekly 'hour' of study of the Bible. (The
participants were labelled 'Stundists', from the German
word for 'hour'.) Thirdly, the government's introduction of
conscription provoked the Mennonites who were pacifists.
Fourthly, the Orthodox Church had become alarmed by the
multiplication of Protestant groups of various kinds. The
result was that in the 1880s many nonconformists were
arrested, fined, imprisoned or exiled to Siberia. Punishing
people for religious 'offences' was not introduced to Russia
by the Bolsheviks but was long established under the Tsars!

'Stundism' was initially a pietistic movement *within* the
Orthodox Church. Although later many of them came to
abandon the sacraments, the priesthood, and the veneration
of the saints, the majority kept their icon corners in their
homes and continued to claim to be Orthodox. In 1868 a
sympathetic provincial governor reported to St Petersburg

that four Stundists had appealed to him for protection against harassment by Orthodox clergy. He wrote that they were good men and 'sober workers', and that the real cause of their troubles was that the village priests were ill-trained, poorly-paid, and had 'a fatal tendency towards alcohol'. Inevitably the relative prosperity of the Stundists was envied by their less hard-working neighbours.

Stundism was often spread by mobile groups of agricultural workers who travelled from place to place in harvest time before mechanical reapers were introduced. Often their only textbook was the Bible, of which a complete translation into Russian was published in 1875 and distributed by energetic colporteurs of the Bible Society. Sects proliferated in the Ukraine. Vasili G. Pavlov, born in 1854 into a Molokan family, was a typical leader. He was converted by reading a Protestant tract at the age of sixteen. A born linguist, he was sent to Hamburg to study under Oncken and returned to Tiflis as a Baptist pastor in 1880. Pobedonostev had him exiled for four years, but he refused to stop preaching and gathered a congregation of one hundred and fifty in his place of exile! Thereafter he was periodically imprisoned for breaking the law against proselytism, i.e. persuading Orthodox to become Baptists. It was no wonder that members of the Holy Synod saw Protestantism as a hydra-headed enemy!

In 1873 another 'outbreak' began in the improbable setting of fashionable drawing-rooms in St Petersburg. This time the initiative came from a Plymouth Brother named Granville Waldegrave, later Lord Radstock. He had experienced an evangelical conversion at the time of the Crimean war. On the invitation of the Countess Chartkova and Princess Lieven he addressed meetings in the palaces of the aristocracy during two winters. Eventually a congregation of 'Evangelical Christians' was formed under the leadership of Princess Lieven's wealthy brother-in-law, Colonel Pashkoff. He tried hard to unite the various Protestant movements, and in 1884 he even convened a conference of Baptists and Evangelicals from all over the country. But the conference was broken up by the police; many of the leaders were exiled to Siberia, and Colonel Pashkoff was forced to go abroad.

Indeed as a result of the assassination of Tsar Alexander in 1881 and the appointment of Konstantin Pobedonostev as Ober-procurator (see page 30 above), the laws against attempts to convert Orthodox church members to any other form of Christianity were intensified. In 1894 a fresh decree forbade Stundist meetings and allowed the police to remove their children from Stundist parents and put them in the charge of Orthodox relatives. Orthodox landowners were forbidden to employ Stundists. Several thousand were transported to Transcaucasia or Siberia. At the same time many Mennonites left their homes on the Dnieper and migrated to Siberia or emigrated to North America in the hope of escaping from the hostilities of Church and state.

But though there were such heavy pressures on the Protestants, Johann Oncken's prophecy was fulfilled. The Protestant congregations continued to grow. New leaders arose to replace the old. Another young man from a Molokan family, I. S. Prokhanoff (1869–1935) experienced an evangelical conversion in 1887. He was able to study at the Baptist College in Bristol in 1895 and 1896. Y. I. Zhidkov (1884–1970) who later became known throughout the world as the representative of the Russian Baptists, grew up in the home of a Bible Society colporteur in Kharkov. Leo Tolstoy became interested in the spiritual revival among the Molokans, and wrote his novel *Resurrection* under their influence. It is the story of a man's attempt to live on the basis of a literal application of the Sermon on the Mount, and one critic described it as a 'nine hundred page tract'. (It is in truth a rather tedious work!)

But pressures on the Protestant minorities varied greatly from year to year and from place to place, and in 1901 Vasili Pavlov was active in St Petersburg. The Russian defeat by Japan in 1905 led to promises of greater religious freedom, some of which were supported by Orthodox churchmen such as Metropolitan Anthony (see page 36 above). A decree of 17 April 1905 actually recognized the right of Orthodox Christians to join other Churches. Later the same year Russian Baptists were represented at the first Baptist World Congress. They reported that there were twenty to twenty-three thousand baptized members of the Baptist Church in Russia at that time.

In 1908 the 'Evangelical Christians' also were able to form a National Union for 'the reformation of Russia by means of individual moral regeneration'. At their first national congress in 1910 it was found that thirty-two of the eighty-six delegates had suffered imprisonment for their faith. In 1909 Baron Paul Nikolai started the Russian Student Christian Movement after visits to St Petersburg and Moscow by John R. Mott. The SCM included Orthodox and Protestant members and after the war it had considerable influence among Russian émigrés. In 1910 a great meeting-place for Evangelical worship, the Dom Evangelia, was built in St Petersburg, and a training school for evangelists was opened.

But such Protestant advances aroused the fears of more reactionary members of the Orthodox Church, and various measures of control were proposed or enacted which were used after the 1917 Revolution against the Orthodox themselves. Police attended services and reported 'subversive' sermons. Magistrates' licences were required for all religious gatherings (except those under Orthodox auspices). The government even passed a regulation forbidding Protestants to organize special meetings for children.

Fortunately in many areas the civic authorities did not enforce these measures. However, when war was declared in 1914 a wave of anti-German feeling swept the country, and as all Protestants were popularly presumed to be Germans, Evangelical movements tended to fall under suspicion. Some of their leaders, including Alexander Karev (1894–1971), who later became secretary of the Baptist Union, were imprisoned.

The Bolshevik Revolution, which drastically changed the situation of the Orthodox Church, at first brought considerable benefits to Baptists and Evangelicals. I have heard them refer to 1918 to 1928 as a 'golden decade'. Exiled preachers like Pavlov were able to return. The Communists' declaration on the separation of Church and state conformed to Baptist principles. No obstacles were put in the way of organizing meetings and gathering congregations. Considerable revivals occurred – for example, as far afield as Omsk.

The Union of Evangelical Christians was greatly strengthened. Until 1924 *Licht im Osten* was able to send in large quantities of Bibles. Twenty-five thousand Bibles were printed in Leningrad in 1927. Several books of psalms, hymns and spiritual songs were published in large editions. A Bible School in Leningrad trained seventy candidates a year for several years. I. S. Prokhanoff said that 'inasmuch as we saw social and economic reforms in the revolution, we welcomed it. To some extent we saw in it God's judgement on the guilty, or we considered it as a purification out of which Russia would come forth renewed.' The Russian delegation to the Baptist World Congress in Toronto in 1928 reported that by then there were two hundred thousand baptized Baptists, with three thousand preachers and over one thousand meeting-houses. (Compared with 1908 this represented a tenfold increase.)

But in 1928 Stalin's first Five Year Plan included 'the unification of thought of all Soviet citizens'. The next year new laws covering all religious activities forbade religious propaganda, Christian charities, and the organization of meetings for women and children. Rents on church buildings were savagely increased. Pastors were deprived of civil rights. The Bible School for preachers was closed. The Baptist Union was dissolved. The Dom Evangelia and the central Baptist church in Moscow were closed. Fifty thousand Bibles were confiscated. In a word the full force of the Communist Party's anti-religious policy, under which the Orthodox Church had suffered so severely for the previous ten years, was suddenly turned against the Baptists and Evangelicals also. Their usefulness to the atheists as 'enemies' of the Orthodox had come to an end. Their success in attracting young people was now recognized by the party as constituting a serious threat to the Marxist world-view.

So the Soviets began to enforce their own version of the theory that only one religion or philosophy should be permitted in a nation-state. The call was for one country (the leader of the worldwide Communist revolution), one Party (the Bolsheviks), one leader (Stalin), and one atheistic philosophy of life (Marxism). So we now turn to the attempt to eradicate Christianity in any form from the USSR

PART TWO

Christians in the USSR

7

The Bolshevik Offensive 1917–1941

Why were the Bolsheviks so fiercely opposed to the Orthodox Church? In the very first weeks after their seizure of power, when they faced a multitude of political and military crises they nevertheless took time to issue a whole series of decrees disestablishing the Church, confiscating its property, secularizing church schools, and depriving the Church of its right to exist as a legal entity. Within four years, twenty-eight bishops and as many as twelve hundred priests had been executed on charges of anti-Soviet activity. Subsequently many thousands more were incarcerated in prisons or penal labour camps. Throughout the past seventy years the Communist Party has continued to oppose all religious organizations – Christian, Jewish, Muslim or Buddhist – and, though there have been intermissions in practice, the fundamental anti-religious laws of the early years still remain in force in the Soviet Union.

There are two main reasons for this enmity. The first is that the Bolsheviks inherited the aggressive atheism of the Russian intelligentsia reinforced by Marxist materialist philosophy. Religion is regarded as being not only an illusion, but also as a most serious obstacle to scientific and material progress. Lenin himself wrote to Maxim Gorky in 1913 denouncing 'every religious idea, every idea of God, even flirting with the idea of God' as being 'unutterable vileness of the most degrading kind, a contagion of the most abominable type'.

The second reason was the close historical association of the Orthodox Church with the Tsarist state. Had not Peter the Great turned the Church into the state 'Department of the Orthodox Confession'? It is easy to see why Lenin's letter continued: 'Every defence or justification of God, even the most refined or the best intentioned, is a *justification of reaction*.' Thus it was inevitable that in the first precarious years of the Soviet regime, the Church should have been regarded as a dangerous potential focus of counter-revolutionary activity.

For much of those seventy years, especially between 1918 and 1922, 1927 and 1941 and 1959 and 1965, hostility to religious faith and organizations was openly and violently expressed. At other times, such as the period of the New Economic Policy after 1922, and during the Second World War and the post-war period 1941 to 1959, hostility towards the Churches was less openly manifested. Sometimes, as in the thirties and under Khrushchev in the early sixties, immense resources were put into atheistic propaganda. At other times, most notably during the war, little was heard of organizations like the League of Militant Godless, and external Soviet propaganda sought to persuade foreigners that 'religious freedom' was guaranteed in the USSR. For long periods leaders of the Churches were personally inhibited by imprisonment or by administrative measures. At other times the government had its own reasons for coming to terms with them and allowing them to appear in public. But the basic expectation of the Party has always been that, when Communism is completely in force, every trace of 'superstition' will have been eliminated. Tactical considerations, such as the need to soothe public opinion in the West, may temporarily lighten the pressures on the Churches, but the objective remains that of hastening their inevitable disappearance.

It is difficult in 1988 to recall that in 1917 it was by no means certain that the Reds would continue to rule for long or be able to extend their authority over the whole country. During the many months of civil war which followed the Bolsheviks' eviction of the Provisional Government, Winston Churchill and other Western politicians thought that with some help from the West the White armies would win. This was the political situation which was developing only a few weeks after the Sobor or National Council of the Russian Orthodox Church began to meet in Moscow in August 1917. They had to choose between three possible responses to the Soviet attacks. The first was all-out opposition to the atheistic anti-imperialist Soviet regime. The second was to regard

Soviet policies as a step in the direction of the establishment of the kingdom of heaven on earth. The third was to recognize the Bolshevik government as 'the power' to which obedience was due 'according to the Scriptures', while continuing to oppose Marxism as a philosophy.

Inevitably the first reaction of the majority in the Sobor favoured the first course. Tikhon, newly elected Patriarch, replied to the anti-church decrees published by Lenin by pronouncing an anathema on the Bolsheviks for 'persecuting the Church of Christ' and for 'daily and in a bestial manner destroying innocent people'. Lenin riposted by disenfranchising the clergy as 'servants of the bourgeoisie' and depriving them of their ration cards.

Tikhon later modified his stance, but Archbishop Anthony Khrapovitsky, the very gifted prelate who had received the most votes in the preliminary election of candidates for the Patriarchate, continued to support the restoration of the Tsardom. Later he supported the 'White' counter-revolutionary forces and eventually had to take refuge in Yugoslavia. There he set up a synod at Karlovcy which claimed to represent the authentic Russian Orthodox Church. Anthony denounced any support for the godless political regime in Russia as being unacceptable to the Christian conscience. When Tikhon, after imprisonment, exhorted the faithful to recognize the Soviet government, Anthony denounced him for betraying the Church. For many years a vociferous section of the Russian emigration supported Anthony. Their determined hostility to the Soviet state undoubtedly increased the difficulties of the Church inside the USSR. Indeed, Metropolitan Nikolai, the chief architect of the *de facto* agreement beween Church and State which lasted from 1943 to 1959, wrote that the 'age-long habit of regarding Orthodoxy as being inseverably connected with the Tsar's rule, had fatal consequences. Even now [i.e. in 1942] one may meet people who honestly cannot understand how we can claim to adhere to the Orthodox Faith considering that we have rejected the Tsar.'

A smaller group of members of the 1917 Sobor directly opposed Archbishop Anthony and publicly welcomed the Soviet Revolution. They included few notable figures, but

57

their leader, the married priest Alexander Vvedensky, established a close relationship with Grigory Zenoviev, the Bolshevik Party chief in Petrograd. In 1922 there was government backing for an attempt by Vvedensky's Renovationist Party to replace Tikhon as head of the Church.

By September 1918 Tikhon had in fact abandoned his initial policy of defiance and had told the clergy to keep out of politics altogether. But this stand did not satisfy the government, and the Kremlin seems to have decided to discredit the Patriarch by taking advantage of a conflict over famine relief. When, as a result of civil war and the fragmentation of the great agricultural estates, famine struck what had been the 'grain basket of Europe', the Patriarch set up a Commission to succour the starving, and offered all the gold and silver objects still in the possession of the Church to be sold abroad in exchange for wheat. He only exempted chalices and other vessels actually used in the Liturgy, but he said that the parishes would contribute funds equivalent to the value of the vessels they retained. However the government saw an opportunity to arouse indignation against the Patriarch for indifference to the fate of the starving, and ordered the seizure of *all* valuable objects still held by the Church. Tikhon banned the surrender of the sacred vessels, and many congregations resisted their removal. As a result fifty-four churchmen were tried on the charge that, by proclaiming church valuables to be inviolate, they had incited the people to engage in civil strife. Several bishops, including the popular young Metropolitan Benjamin of Petrograd, were found guilty and executed; many priests were condemned to be shot or imprisoned on the same charge, and the Patriarch himself was arrested.

In this crisis the Renovationists occupied the patriarchal chancellery; the majority of the bishops who were still free were induced to support their administration, and twenty thousand church buildings were handed over to them by the state. It was said that only four of the four hundred churches still 'working' in Moscow outwardly supported Tikhon, but it soon became clear that the overwhelming majority of the faithful would not accept the Renovationists' policies. Nevertheless the government enabled them to call a new

Sobor, which met in April 1923 with four hundred and seventy-six members. The Sobor passed resolutions of support for Lenin, rescinded Tikhon's anathema, excommunicated the members of the Karlovcy Synod, recognized married bishops and the right of widowed priests to remarry, tried Tikhon in his absence for his reactionary policies, and stripped him of his patriarchal office and monastic status.

However the government had by this time lost confidence in the Renovationists, and there had been strong pressure for the Patriarch's release both by the Archbishop of Canterbury and by the governments of countries from which the Soviets needed to obtain grain. So only a month after the meeting of the Sobor, Tikhon was unexpectedly released. But there was a *quid pro quo*. He had to publish a confession that because he had been 'raised in monarchical society and exposed to the influence of anti-soviet circles' he had 'succumbed to a negative attitude to Soviet power'. He disavowed any connection with counter-revolutionary movements (such as the Karlovcy Synod) at home or abroad.

Two years later an even stronger statement was issued over his signature while he lay dying. In it he called upon the clergy to permit no anti-government activity, to nourish no hopes of the return of the Tsardom and to recognize the Soviet government. He affirmed that the fate of nations was determined by God, and called upon Christians to accept what had happened as God's will for Russia. 'Without transgressing against our faith and our Church, without any compromises in doctrine' Christians should be loyal to the Soviet power, adapt to the new structures of the state, and condemn any open or secret agitation against it.

Inevitably émigrés denounced this 'testament' as a forgery, but there is evidence that it was genuine. Metropolitan Peter Polyansky, with Tikhon when he was on his deathbed, believed that such a declaration of loyalty would free the Patriarchate to deal with the Renovationist usurpation, restore order in the Church, and improve relations with the state. But the government's response was not favourable. Metropolitan Peter, who had been prudently nominated as *locum tenens*, together with the first two bishops he himself had nominated as his successors, were imprisoned. Only his

Patriarch Sergius

third choice, Metropolitan Sergius of Nizhni Novgorod, eventually succeeded in taking over responsibility.

Sergius Stragordsky is such an important figure in the recent history of the Russian Church, and his relations with the Soviet state aroused such violent criticisms, both from emigrés at the time and later from respected prophets of 'Orthodox Dissent', that it is useful to recall the course of his ecclesiastical career. He had been a missionary in Japan, a chaplain in the embassy in Athens, rector of the Theological Academy at St Petersburg, author of a major theological work on the Orthodox Doctrine of Salvation, chairman of the 'Religious-Philosophical' meetings between theologians and members of the intelligentsia in 1901 (see page 37), and a supporter of the workers' priest, Fr Gapon, in 1904. As Archbishop of Finland (then part of the Russian Empire) he welcomed the imperial edict of toleration for Old Believers and Protestants in 1905, and served on the Commission which worked out proposals for reform for the Sobor which met at last in 1917. His friends maintained that, after the Revolution, his primary concern was to preserve the existence and unity and canonical order of the Church in the Soviet state. This explains why he joined the Renovationists for a short time (most of which he spent under arrest), and then sought reconciliation with Tikhon as soon as the Patriarch was released from prison.

When he became *locum tenens* in 1925 he stated that he would seek some degree of legalization for the Church, including the right to reopen seminaries, have a canonical administration and publish some literature. As a first step he applied for 'registration' in line with Tikhon's initiatives. But in the autumn of 1926 he was re-arrested, allegedly for conniving at a secret poll of the bishops for the election of a Patriarch. Three months after his release he issued his notorious 'Declaration of Loyalty' to the Soviet state.

What did he actually write? He blamed the anti-Soviet pronouncements of the Karlovcy Synod for the delay in normalizing relations with the state. He thanked the government for promising to allow a provisional synod to be organized. He expressed the hope that dioceses and parishes would soon be legalized and that a Patriarch would be elected. And then he went on to affirm that 'the most fervent adherents of Orthodoxy can be faithful citizens of the Soviet Union, loyal to the Soviet government . . . The Soviet Union is our motherland, whose joys and sorrows are our joys and sorrows, whose misfortunes are our misfortunes' (the relative pronoun 'whose' agreed with the feminine 'motherland', not with the masculine 'Soviet Union'). He cited St Paul's exhortation to obey the rulers of the Roman Empire 'not from fear but for conscience' sake' (Rom. 13.5), and ended with a request to émigré clergy to pledge loyalty to the Soviet government as the effective rulers of Russia.

The main charges brought against Sergius and his successors by their critics in the Church were, first, that they had entered into any kind of deal with the atheist rulers of the USSR; second, that they had agreed to co-operate with the secret police; third, that they had repeatedly lied to foreigners and insulted those who were suffering as martyrs by asserting that 'religious liberty' existed in the USSR; and fourth, in retrospect, that the concessions they had made to the state may have secured some temporary benefits for the bishops who conformed but made no worthwhile or lasting improvements in the situation of the faithful.

Orthodox writers who defend Sergius (and those who followed his line) claim that he was extremely adroit in defending the faith under appallingly difficult conditions (which included Stalin's reign of terror); that his diplomatic skill and foresight preserved in existence an embryonic form of church organization ready to emerge from the catacombs in 1943; and that he cannot be held responsible for the failure of the Soviet authorities to keep their side of the bargains he made with them. In the judgement of W. F. Fletcher, one of the most respected writers on the Church in the USSR, 'if Metropolitan Sergius had not found some means of tempering the adamant hostility of the Soviet state, it is doubtful whether the Church could have continued to exist much beyond 1927 as an institution in Soviet society.' After his first meeting with Sergius in 1943, the Archbishop of York, Cyril Garbett, reminded his chaplains that Jesus called upon his followers to be 'wise as serpents' as well as 'innocent as doves'.

If Sergius expected that his Declaration of Loyalty would lead to some relaxation of the pressures on the Church, his hopes were not fulfilled in 1927. Only insignificant and short-lived concessions were made, and the process of eliminating the outward expressions of church life went on remorselessly. The new regulations on religious associations codified in 1929 required 'registration' of all religious groups (i.e. congregations). Any kind of organized teaching of religion in schools or in private was prohibited. Religious groups were made responsible for the maintenance, taxes and insurance (often fixed at arbitrary levels) on 'prayer buildings' they leased from local authorities. The proceeds of collections could be used exclusively for the maintenance of the building and the salaries of the clergy. Any kind of charitable or educational work was prohibited. Permission to use a building for worship would be withdrawn if the membership of the sponsoring group fell below twenty (which could easily result from arrest or exile), and local authorities could resume use of the premises at any time for social purposes. At the same time, an amendment of the Constitution which proclaimed 'freedom of religion and of anti-religious propaganda' was interpreted as prohibiting any attempt to persuade workers or children to become believers.

Two other actions by the government greatly increased pressure on the Churches in these years. The first was the support given to the League of Militant Godless. This claimed to have a membership of five million in 1932, and to have published over one hundred and forty million items of anti-religious propaganda between 1928 and 1940. For several years every school, trade union branch and social club had to arrange classes in atheism, and the pressure on boys and girls to join Communist youth organizations which practised the 'Lenin cult' was intense.

But Stalin's policy of enforced agricultural collectivization in the early thirties had even more serious consequences for the Church. Many millions of peasants died of starvation or in the penal work-camps, and many thousands of village communities were destroyed or had their churches turned into barns, garages or social clubs. The patriarchal *locum tenens*, living in a country cottage outside Moscow with little contact with the few bishops remaining in their dioceses, had no means of collecting reliable statistics, but from reports in the Soviet press and publications of the Militant Godless observers estimate that the total number of churches open for worship fell from around thirty thousand in 1930 to a thousand at most in 1940.

In Moscow, with a population of eight million, only fifteen of the four hundred churches were still open for worship. Many of the rest had been destroyed. Only five were still 'working' in Leningrad in 1941, and the great Kazan cathedral there had been turned into an anti-religious museum, as had a number of churches in other cities. The great sea-port of Odessa, with half a million people, had only one church open for worship – and that had no regular priest. In many considerable towns no churches were open. A rough comparison could be made with a medium-sized English city such as Leeds, with a population of three-quarters of a million. At present it is served by 177 churches or chapels. Under a Soviet regime the Roman Catholic cathedral might have become an anti-God museum. The great parish church would have been blown up for a motor-way approach, and only three Anglican churches (out of 71), one Roman Catholic church (out of 37), one Free Church (out of 69), and one synagogue would still have been open.

The available figures for the number of 'working' clergy were equally disastrous. In 1930 there were still nearly sixty thousand (including Renovationists and other schismatics); but by 1940 the number of those officially in the service of the Church as priests was probably down to around three thousand (excluding clergy in the territories occupied in 1939). Thousands had been executed on charges of anti-Soviet activities, and many more had died in prisons or work-camps. Some observers put the total of priests who died at 45,000. A decree of 1932 prohibited 'non-workers' (including priests) from residing in the larger cities, and another decree evicted clergy from 'nationalized housing' which of course included former parish houses. 'Missionary journeys' by priests to serve churches where there was no longer a priest were forbidden. Salaries paid to priests were subject to exorbitant taxation, and clergy were forbidden to earn extra money in subsidiary employments. In fact, if these anti-clerical measures had been applied consistently over the whole country the parochial clergy would have disappeared completely. As it was, the ratio of officially registered clergy to the total population in the territory of pre-1939 Russia probably fell as low as one to one hundred and fifty thousand.

There had been 63 dioceses served by 163 bishops before 1914. By 1940 nearly all were either dead, in prison or living under the harshest conditions in the lethal work-camps in Northern Russia or Siberia. Only a handful were still free. One of them graphically compared their situation to that of chickens in a shed from which the cook snatched her victims at will.

It was therefore not surprising that Soviet officials and many outside observers concluded that when the generation of pre-1917 believers had died off all traces of religion would have been eliminated. Soviet publicists did their work so well that when the Archbishop of York returned from Moscow in 1943 Western journalists expressed doubts about the continued existence of any genuine Christians in the Soviet Union, and when the Archbishop described the crowded services he had attended it was repeatedly suggested that he had been the victim of a gigantic confidence trick mounted by the secret police.

Nevertheless, the Church did survive those bitter years, and not only 'underground'. In 1943 the Patriarch and his colleagues assured Archbishop Garbett that Russia was still a 'Christian country' in the sense that the majority even of those born since 1917 had been baptized. 'The grand-mothers had done their duty!' As the pro-Soviet writer Maurice Hindus observed in 1943, 'In Russia the grand-mothers are the real nurses of the children. If they are religious, as nearly all of them are, they naturally seek to instil their own faith into their grandchildren.' He added bitterly, 'Often they succeed only too well.' In city churches baptisms by immersion were administered daily at all seasons of the year in side-chapels which were heated in winter. Many witnesses testify that the few churches still open for

worship in the cities continued to be crammed with worshippers at services held three times a day every day of the week.
(Stalin had replaced the seven-day week by one of ten days.)
Many priests had monks driven from their parishes and
monasteries, and deprived (until 1936) of civil rights and
ration cards travelled from village to village in the more
remote areas and baptized, instructed, heard confessions,
prayed and gave blessings clandestinely. Groups of nuns
were attached to parishes. Some ordinands were trained in
the homes of bishops or priests. (The fact that the village
priesthood had largely become hereditary was a positive
advantage under these conditions.) An unknown number of
small secret monasteries were set up in remote places –
especially in Siberia. The faith of many households was
sustained by the centuries-old custom of gathering the
family for prayer in the icon-corner.

Although organized church life did not cease completely
the great majority of believers suffered exceedingly. It is
almost impossible for comfortably-situated western Christians like us to enter imaginatively into the desolating
experiences of Christians in the USSR when Stalin was
exerting maximum pressure on the people and the Churches.
A novel such as Boris Pasternak's *Doctor Zhivago* (not the
film) vividly evokes the deprivations and frustrations of the
earlier part of the period. How many beloved members of
other families just disappeared in the time of the great purges
as Lara did?

> One day Lara went out and did not come back. She must have
> been arrested in the street, as so often happened in those days,
> and she died or vanished somewhere, forgotten as a nameless
> number on a list that was mislaid, in one of the innumerable
> concentration camps in the north. (chapter 15)

In *One Day in the Life of Ivan Denisovich*, Alexander
Solzhenitsyn paints an unforgettable picture of life in a penal
work-camp, and the first part of his *Gulag Archipelago*
chronicles how individuals, families and whole companies of
people were sucked into what he calls 'our sewage disposal
system', the terrors of which hung over every ordinary
citizen.

Even outside the camps it was a desperate struggle in those days to find the minimum amount of food, clothes and shelter needed to keep alive. Then imagine that one morning as you go down the road to work you see that the church in which you and your family have worshipped for generations has been blown up, or had its iconostasis and furniture removed, its bells taken away to be melted down and the crosses torn off, so that it can be used as a youth club or warehouse. Next you learn that your parish priest has been arrested along with several leading members of the congregation. You yourself may be the next to go. In such circumstances, psalms and anthems which you have heard sung for many years, perhaps without much personal meaning, suddenly come alive. 'But now they break down all the carved work thereof with axes and hammers' (Psalm 74.7). 'The snares of death compassed me about and the pains of hell got hold upon me' (Psalm 18.4, Antiphon I for Palm Sunday). Then comes the assurance, 'Thou calledst me in trouble, and I delivered thee: and heard thee when the storm fell upon thee' (Psalm 81.7).

There is evidence that numerous Russian Christians were sustained in their trials by memories of the Liturgy. Whenever they had the opportunity they crowded into the few churches which still remained open, or at least joined the immense crowds which thronged round them on major festivals.

Lenin himself acknowledged the truth of the observation that 'the blood of the martyrs is the seed of the Church', and he vainly warned his followers against creating martyrs by open persecution. On their side many Russian Christians, in the spirit of saints Boris and Gleb (see page 7 above), felt the call to follow Christ in his humiliation, suffering and death.

Thus providentially it came about that when, under the stress of the German invasion, Stalin somewhat lightened the extremely severe pressure on the Orthodox Church, there was still a substantial body of faithful worshippers in Russia ready to respond. The Russian Phoenix was awaiting the call to rise from the ashes.

8
The Phoenix Rises 1941–1959

German Panzer divisions invaded Russia in June 1941 and advanced at a terrifying speed. In the Kremlin many succumbed to panic. But on the very first Sunday after the invasion Metropolitan Sergius, as Guardian of the Patriarchal throne, issued a stirring call to all Christians to fight for the defence of their country. He celebrated the Liturgy for a densely packed congregation and led special prayers for the victory of the Russian army. In his sermon he recalled previous occasions on which Russian Christians had fought for their native land, for their historic sanctuaries and for freedom from a foreign yoke. He affirmed that the Orthodox Church had always shared the nation's fate at such times of crisis. 'Christ's Church blesses all Orthodox members defending the sacred borders of the fatherland. God will grant us victory!' In a notable passage in a sermon on a subsequent Sunday he called upon Christians to pray for *all* who gave their lives on the battlefield, irrespective of whether 'they were cooling towards religion or even denouncing it'.

The Metropolitan's patriotic appeal was echoed in the Orthodox Churches still open for worship. Vast numbers of the faithful responded by attending services which had to be repeated two or three times a day in city churches every day of the week. This spontaneous reaction was all the more remarkable in view of the fact that Nazi propaganda was loudly proclaiming that the invaders aimed to liberate Christians from persecution by the atheistic Soviet regime. In fact a small number of churchmen, especially in territories annexed by the USSR in 1940, did align themselves with the invaders. The best known was Metropolitan Sergius Voskresensky, who calculated that the best hope of the Church for the future lay in a German victory. He was eventually assassinated. But the great majority of the surviving church

A crowded cathedral in wartime

leaders and the overwhelming mass of believers supported the patriotic cause.

As the situation of the Russian armies became more and more desperate, with hundreds of thousands taken prisoner or killed and the Panzer divisions within fifteen miles of Moscow on the west and threatening to cut the city off from the east, the Kremlin began to relax pressure on the Church. The publications of the League of Militant Godless were suspended 'in order to save paper'. During the winter the number of churches open for worship in Moscow rose from fourteen to forty. At Easter 1942, in response to massive popular demand, the curfew was lifted in the city so that worshippers could attend the traditional midnight services. (Moscow was bombed much less severely than London.) About the same time a leading Soviet official was quoted in the *New York Times* as acknowledging that 'religious faith is part and parcel of the Russian national make-up'.

Sir John Lawrence, at that time press attaché at the British Embassy and editor of the very successful weekly paper *British Ally*, wrote in his book *Russians Observed* (1969) that while Pasternak was the only member of the intelligentsia who openly confessed an interest in Christianity, there were numerous believers among the simple people. The Kremlin recognized the absolute necessity of unity in face of the enemy, so persecution was suspended and religion tolerated even in the army. When the Communist Party in Kuibyshev protested to the government that religion was being tolerated even though it was known to be false, the official reply was that 'experience had shown that a man who had religious faith was likely to be a better soldier'.

Lawrence also recorded his first unexpected encounter with leaders of the Russian Church. One day in 1942, fourteen months after the invasion, two bearded gentlemen turned up at the British Embassy carrying parcels. (No Russian citizen could visit a foreign Mission except under the direction of the Kremlin.) Once inside they undid the parcels and robed themselves in the cassocks and head-dresses of Orthodox bishops. One of them was Metropolitan Nikolai Yarushevich, Sergius' right-hand man. They discussed relations with the Church of England. After their

Metropolitan Nikolai

interview with the diplomats they disrobed, packed up their parcels and emerged on to the street as civilians.

In November, Nikolai was appointed to serve on the 'Extraordinary State Commission of Inquiry into German Crimes in Occupied Territories', and he had a major part in the publication of a strange book entitled *The Truth about Religion in Russia*. It was sumptuously produced on the presses which had belonged to the Church before 1917, but which had printed atheistic propaganda from 1925 to 1941. The contents were mostly patriotic sermons and declarations of loyalty by church leaders to the Soviet government. There were contentious assertions that the Church was 'free'.

The main message of the book was summarized in a pamphlet, *The Russian Church and the War against Fascism*, which was widely circulated in several languages. Some quotations illustrate its character. Nikolai wrote: 'In October 1917 a new page in the history of Russia was opened. By the will of the Russian people the government of the Soviets was set up. In this critical period the Russian Church remained true to its historical tradition: it was united with the people. It recognized the Soviet regime as established by God and expressing the will of the people.' He stated unequivocally that the Soviet's proclamation of freedom of conscience ensured 'for every religious community the right to exist and to conduct its religious affairs in conformity with the requirements of its faith'. (This was only correct if the 'requirements' of the Orthodox Church were confined to the extremely narrow limits imposed by the state.)

According to Nikolai, Soviet decrees had helped the Church to rid itself of its subordination to the Tsarist regime and to become self-governing and self-supporting. He admitted that the clergy and the monasteries had been deprived of certain rights and privileges, but he thought that church-goers regarded these changes 'not as a persecution but as a return to apostolic times'. He acknowledged that the Church had sustained considerable losses in membership, but he explained that this was the result of the removal of barriers which had 'artificially kept the people within the Church's fold'. Clergymen had been prosecuted because they had engaged in anti-Soviet political activities.

The booklet was a typical propaganda piece directed both to the Soviet government and to the Christian public in the West. Undoubtedly it contributed to the prevalent confusion of Western observers between real 'freedom of religion' and a very limited degree of 'freedom of religious worship'. But when Metropolitan Nikolai talked privately about conditions in the Church before 1941 he did not suggest that everything had been perfect. He never said anything negative that might have been quoted against him by the censors, but much of what he said about his hopes for the reconstruction of church life after the war assumed that his hearers knew a good deal about the real state of the Church before the war. For example, speaking of plans for ministering to the people in the villages (where two-thirds of the population were still living in 1939), he did not refer directly to closed churches, but he said that the Church's aim was to begin by providing a priest for each group of five or so villages.

Meanwhile in Leningrad, where 650,000 people perished in the siege, his colleague Metropolitan Alexis Simansky was earning public approval for sustaining the morale of the people both by refusing to accept possibilities of escaping from the city and by his preaching. When Easter Day coincided with the seven hundredth anniversary of Alexander Nevski's victory over the Teutonic Knights on the ice of Lake Peipus, he made the parallel with the Nazi German invasion in 1941. He repeatedly affirmed that the great heroes of Russian military history, Alexander Nevski and Dmitri Donskoi, had won their victories thanks to the faith of the Russian people that God would defend their just cause. He also pioneered the practice of inviting the congregations to make donations for the support of army units. He thought it was faithless to abandon a Liturgy when the German artillery started to shell the city, and on one occasion an entire congregation were killed by a direct hit. Their deaths were regarded as a kind of martyrdom.

But although the church leaders gave such immediate outspoken support for the war effort, Stalin was cautious about making any substantial concessions. For instance, it was not until January 1943, eighteen months after the invasion, that the Church obtained permission to open a bank account for the funds donated for the armed forces; but the permission to open this account implied a significant *de facto* recognition of the Church as a legal entity for the first time since 1917. In the following months more bishops were liberated, more churches were opened for worship, and a secret invitation to visit Moscow was sent through diplomatic channels to the Archbishop of Canterbury.

Two years after the German invasion Stalin at last took dramatic public action concerning the Church. Sergius, Nikolai and Alexis were brought to Moscow on 3 September 1943. To his surprise Sergius was not taken to the modest cottage on the outskirts of the city where he had lived before the war, but was installed in the imposing former residence of the German ambassador. The next day the three Metropolitans were driven to the Kremlin to be received by Stalin and Molotov.

Various accounts have been given of this historic meeting. According to one account Molotov began by saying that the Soviet government, and Stalin personally, wanted to know 'what the Church needed'. Sergius said that they wanted to open many more churches, to be able to train priests and to hold a Sobor for the election of a Patriarch. Stalin asked why there was a shortage of clergy. (In fact, it was because so many had perished in the camps.) Sergius replied that one reason was that 'when a man had been trained in a seminary he became a marshal of the Soviet Union'. Stalin is said to have enjoyed this joke and to have gone on reminiscing about his years in a Georgian seminary until three o'clock in the morning. However that may be, it seems that the main lines of the future settlement for the Church were approved in the course of this interview. According to another account, Stalin assisted the aged Sergius down the steps saying, 'Your Grace, this is all I can do for you at the present time.'

Substantial results became visible immediately. Shortly afterwards nineteen bishops were allowed to meet and constitute a Synod. They unanimously elected Sergius as Patriarch. Soon more churches were opened. The Church was given permission to publish a journal and promised that seminaries would be opened after the war. Even though the legislation against the Church was not withdrawn, actual anti-religious activities were greatly reduced. The contrast with the position before 1941 was marked.

The secret of Stalin's motives in giving greater breathing-space to the Churches remains locked up in the archives of the Kremlin, together with details of any concessions to the secret police which may have been forced out of the church leaders. But a number of factors were noted at the time which might have motivated Stalin's remarkable reversal of public policy. First in time (though not probably in importance) was the fact that the German invaders had from the start proclaimed that they had come to liberate Christians from persecution by the atheistic Soviet state. Secondly, at a time when Stalin still needed help from the Western allies, it was well known that public opinion, in North America especially, was critical of Soviet attacks on the Churches. Thirdly, the Orthodox populations of the German-occupied countries of south-eastern Europe had traditionally looked to the Moscow Patriarchate for protection, and an apparently freer Church would boost Russian prestige both in the Balkans and in the Near East. But probably the most important consideration was that the Russian people themselves had been under tremendous psychological and social strain. Fifty million were living in the areas occupied by the Nazi forces and the total number killed was mounting towards the horrific figure of twenty million. The government knew that in spite of years of intensive atheistic propaganda and pressure on the Church, millions of Russians were still believers. They also knew that church leaders had given proof of loyalty to the national cause and that it was 'safe' to make the 'consolations of religion' available to larger numbers. So there certainly were a number of good diplomatic, social and even military reasons for reducing the state's pressure on the Church for the time being; but this did not imply that the Party was abandoning its fundamental opposition to religion or that the bishops were not still kept under great but secret pressure.

One striking sign of the change in the public situation of the Church was the fact that when the Archbishop of York arrived by air at Moscow a few days after the election of the Patriarch, he was greeted at the airport by Nikolai and two

75

other dignitaries wearing their traditional robes; by the British Minister, by numerous foreign correspondents and by a unit of the Red Army! After some days his arrival was reported in the Soviet press and he was allowed to publish a message to the Russian people. He was treated with great ceremonial courtesy by the authorities in accordance with pre-1914 protocol. The arrival at the Archbishop's hotel of the Patriarch and his entourage wearing their cassocks and very distinctive head-dresses caused a sensation. One of the hotel staff whispered that he too was a believer.

The two services in the Patriarchal Cathedral which the Archbishop attended were crammed with worshippers – estimated by journalists to number about ten thousand on each occasion. The congregations were very attentive to the Patriarch's words of greeting and to the Archbishop's reply. They sang the Lord's Prayer, the Creed and other responses with great fervour (instead of leaving all the singing to the choir as had been customary in Russia). The silence during the special prayer for victory and the prayers for the departed was intense, and when the Archbishop was on his way out they pressed upon him and tried to touch his robes, calling out, 'Thank you! Thank you!' The congregations in the cathedral – like the crowds on the streets – consisted very largely of women of varied ages and young children; but there were some men, including even a few in uniform. Later, at the Novodevichi Monastery (then a museum), an elderly curator, who had apparently continued working on the restoration of the fine sixteenth-century frescoes even when the German army was only a few miles from the gates of Moscow, said to one of the Archbishop's chaplains, 'The church is very beautiful, but not so beautiful as when services were held here.'

In 1943 security was less strict than on subsequent occasions, and Archbishop Garbett was able to talk with Metropolitan Nikolai with only a British interpreter being present, and one of his chaplains had long conversations in French alone with Metropolitan Alexis. (Some of the material in the previous chapter is based on what was said or hinted at in these conversations and confirmed later from other sources.) It was of course necessary to be discreet and to be prepared

The Archbishop of York, Cyril Garbett, in Moscow, 1943. Patriarch Sergius is on his left.

to read between the lines. For example, when Alexis was asked how many bishops had taken part in the recent election of the Patriarch, he said that nineteen had been present, but added that many others were in Siberia and other places from which it had not been possible for them to travel 'under existing conditions'. It was clear that he knew that his questioner knew that he was not referring only to the difficulties of war-time travel.

Some of the answers received were surprising. For example, when Nikolai was asked about provision for training ordinands after the war, he said that not only was he confident that seminaries would be opened, but also that, in spite of the twenty-year-long ban on all religious publications, they would have plenty of theological reference books, because, when the war began, the Soviet government had carefully despatched 'to the eastern regions' the contents of the great theological libraries of the Academies of Kiev and Moscow. Some other more public assertions may well have been made as part of the secret deal with the Kremlin. For instance, was it really the case that in 1943 'the Church was as freely self-governed as at any time in Russian history'? Or that in future all new bishops would be elected by the Synod

'without any interference from the state'? (The first statement could have been literally true at that particular
moment, but the second represented, at best, a hope which
was not realized.) In any case, the Archbishop's party were
well aware that their visit – and the meeting of the Synod of
bishops for the election of the Patriarch which preceded it –
could have taken place only with Stalin's approval. Soon
afterwards the Kremlin set up a 'Council for the Affairs of
the Orthodox Church'. At first this may have served primarily as a means of meeting requests from the Church, for
example for the supply of materials for the repair of church
buildings; but the Council soon developed into an instrument for increasing state control of the Church.

The ambiguities and uncertainties inevitable in contacts
with Churches in the Soviet Union were illustrated in other
ways. Was another young bishop romanticizing or merely
relaying what he was expected to say when he reported that
peasants brought traditional offerings of bread and salt to
Sergius at country stations when he was being brought back
to Moscow by train? Was it true that the bishop of a large
and inaccessible diocese had been offered the use of a
government aeroplane for pastoral visits in winter? Was the
claim made by another that the Russians were still 'a deeply
religious people' wishful thinking or fact? (Even Communist
writers were complaining that large numbers of babies were
still being baptized.) British diplomats had seen few signs of
anti-religious propaganda since 1941 and it was reported
that no lessons in atheism were being given in schools; on the
other hand a school library well stocked with pictures, charts
and books about scientists, politicians, soldiers, philosophers
and secular events appeared to contain no material on
religion at all – not even anti-religious writings.

Patriarch Sergius was seventy-eight at this time and at
some of the meetings with the Archbishop of York he would
appear to doze off, but he would then intervene with some
very relevant remark. On one occasion the Archbishop was
answering questions about the Church of England's contribution to the war effort. He described national days of
prayer, memorial services and sermons, and discussions
about war aims. But suddenly the Patriarch expressed his

astonishment that the British congregations were not being asked to give money directly for the equipment of the armed forces. He said that in the USSR special collections for the war effort were taken at all the main services, and enough had been given to build and equip a complete tank division named after the warrior saint Dmitri Donskoi. (Later it was reported that a total of one hundred and fifty million roubles had been donated by the Church.)

Such patriotic activities 'earned' the Church some substantial concessions. By the time of Sergius's death in May 1944 considerable progress had been made towards the realization of his aim of restoring order in the Church, particularly by the re-establishment of dioceses and the appointment of bishops. A theological institute for the training of priests had been planned to open in the Novodevichi Convent. Metropolitan Alexis, as *locum tenens*, wrote to Stalin affirming his adherence both to the canons and regulations of the Church and to 'the fatherland and to Stalin as head of the government'. In January 1945 he was able to bring together an episcopal synod of forty-one bishops, which elected him as Patriarch and accorded him much greater authority over the Church than the Sobor of 1917 had envisaged. Here again there is a typical ambiguity. The bishops may have intended to strengthen the Church against renewed attacks, or, as some observers suggest, this may have been a measure enforced on the Church as a means of enabling the Communist Party to exercise greater control over it through the bishops. Were both motives at work?

In any case, the relationship of Church and state set up in 1943 continued for fifteen years under the leadership of Patriarch Alexis and Metropolitan Nikolai, and with the aid of General Georgy Karpov, who presided over the government's Council for Orthodox Church Affairs. During this period there was an astonishing expansion in the visible life of the Church in the Soviet state. The number of church buildings restored and opened for worship rose from a few hundred to between sixteen and twenty thousand. By the end of the period more than twenty thousand priests were functioning legally. The original seventy-four dioceses were at work again under their own bishops. Two major

Metropolitan (later Patriarch) Alexis

academies and eight seminaries were training ordinands, but the demand for priests greatly exceeded the capacity of these institutions, and bishops were ordaining men on condition that they continued to follow correspondence courses for several years. The *Journal of the Patriarchate* was being published together with a few other religious publications and very limited editions of the Bible in Russian. The great monastery of St Sergius and the Holy Trinity at Zagorsk was restored to the Church's use; but in general monastic life continued to be limited to under fifty communities – mostly in the west. Metropolitan Nikolai explained that this was partly because so many congregations preferred monks to married priests. Nikolai himself made several visits to Paris, London and the United States. He organized a very successful tour of the Middle East by Patriarch Alexis which must have considerably enhanced the Church's standing with the Soviet government.

Towards the end of this period, when a Russian bishop was asked what was his most serious problem 'as a bishop', he replied unexpectedly: 'We have too much money'. Worshippers gave very generously, but the Church was only allowed to spend their offerings on the clergy and on the maintenance of church buildings. There could be no charitable, educational or social work, and at this time crushing taxes were not being exacted from the clergy. Consequently, priests serving in city churches were often well paid by Soviet standards, and the consequent danger of corruption was very real. (This may indeed have been what the Soviet authorities were counting on.) This bishop dealt with the problem of 'superfluous wealth' in his parishes by replacing the gold paint on the dome of the cathedral, which frequently needed renewal, by gold leaf, which he said should last for three hundred years! Later, under Khrushchev, he was removed from his diocese on some trumped-up charge.

The personality of Alexis contrasted with the wily diplomacy of Sergius and the managerial skills and personal charm of Nikolai. Many people regarded him as being above all else a man of prayer. He told the Archbishop of York's chaplain that he was convinced that the one and only essential freedom for the Church was freedom to celebrate the Liturgy. This required the opening of church buildings and the training and support of the clergy. Other freedoms enjoyed by other Churches – to evangelize, publish, educate and do charitable works – were desirable but not necessary. Thus at the very end of his life he told an English dean that his one central concern had been to train priests to lead worship. During the last ten years of his long life and twenty-five years as Patriarch he was fiercely attacked by some courageous and sincere priests and laymen in the USSR for failing to stand up to Khrushchev's resumed attacks on the Church. Sad memories of this later period of his patriarchate may have unduly obscured the remarkable record of reconstruction of church life in the preceding fourteen years. Had he died in 1959 he might have been acclaimed as an outstanding leader.

For in 1959, when the new wave of attacks on the Church was beginning, two incidents occurred which appeared to show Alexis acting with remarkable courage. One December morning the Party newspaper *Pravda* carried a long article by Alexander Osipov, who had up till then served as Professor of Old Testament Studies in the Leningrad Theological Academy. In it he announced his apostasy and attacked the unscientific obscurantism of his former colleagues. A few days later the Patriarch publicly excommunicated him for having 'openly slandered the Name of God'. In the circumstances this was a remarkably daring act. Then in February 1960 the Patriarch used the opportunity provided by a meeting in the Kremlin to reply to intensifying public attacks on the Church. He recalled the major role of the Church in the creation of the Russian state, in civilizing the people, and in inspiring resistance to foreign invaders. In view of these facts of Russian history he demanded an end to unjustified attacks on the Church by Party propagandists.

Some observers think that this speech reflected a decision by Metropolitan Nikolai that the time had come to make a public stand. His dismissal in 1960 coincided with a revival of the Communist Party's campaign against religion. What kind of impression did Nikolai make on those who met him during the years when he exercised a major influence on the leadership of the Church, and especially on its relations with the government? Professor Leo Zander of the Institute of St Sergius in Paris summed up his impressions in a letter to Dr Visser 't Hooft, the General Secretary of the World Council of Churches. He wrote that Metropolitan Nikolai was 'intelligent, amiable, obliging, on the young side and full of energy, authoritarian but only within certain limits. He knows what he is saying, and he knows even better what he must not say. One sees in him on the one hand the Orthodox hierarch with all the qualities and gifts which characterize our higher clergy; on the other side one recognizes quite clearly a dignitary of the Soviet state who is bound by obligations of which he pretends to be unaware. The general impression is therefore twofold, but more agreeable than might have been expected.'

Nikolai was deeply involved in the early development of the Moscow-inspired 'Prague Peace Movement'; but his major international achievement was to prepare the way for the Russian Church to join the World Council of Churches. The possibility of this move depended largely on the temperature of Soviet–American relations. Efforts to arrange for the Moscow Patriarchate to take part in the founding Assembly at Amsterdam in 1948 were frustrated by the intensification of the cold war. Nikolai responded to initiatives from the WCC at Evanston in 1955 and Davos in 1956, but these moves were again frustrated by the Hungarian crisis in 1956. However he was eventually able to attend a crucial meeting with officers of the WCC at Utrecht in 1958 and to arrange a visit by a team of WCC staff to the Churches in the Soviet Union in 1959.

So the end of the period of relatively less official oppression of the Russian Church by the Soviet state may be regarded as having been marked by two contrasting events. On 26 November 1961 the Third Assembly of the World Council meeting at New Delhi warmly welcomed the Patriarchal Church into membership; but on 13 December Metropolitan Nikolai died in obscure circumstances in Moscow. Some say that he was poisoned. Many Russians regard him as a martyr for the faith. The truth about his death may never be known. But perhaps he voiced his own memorial when he said to the Archbishop of York in 1943: 'Every Christian has to bear his own cross. My cross is to make the decisions which are necessary if a visible Church is to continue in the Soviet Union.' Many years later, when an official delegation from the British Council of Churches asked to visit Nikolai's tomb, the chapel was found to be unpublicized but in perfect order. Could this be a symbol of the understanding and approbation which he will eventually be accorded?

9
Trials and Triumphs 1959–1988

As he comes nearer the present a foreign writer about events in the USSR becomes more conscious of the difficulty of his task. Hard facts are difficult to confirm and experts differ so widely in their assessments of them. There is general agreement that the Churches came under exceptionally severe pressure in the sixties, but observers of the eighties are less of one mind. All remind us that the fundamental laws severely restricting the activities of the Churches remain in place, together with the far-reaching apparatus of surveillance by the police of the activities of all Soviet citizens. But there appear to have been considerable variations in the application of those laws from time to time and place to place, and some recent developments point towards an easing of the situation for the Churches.

According to an experienced Western observer, in Russia before and after the Revolution 'informers are as numerous and as inconspicuously ever-present as sparrows'. It is exceedingly difficult for any British or American citizen to imagine what it must be like to live under a system in which every block of flats, every hotel room, every office and factory, every student's study, every group travelling abroad and every contact with a foreigner is liable to be observed by a secret informer. For the safety of his family a man might conceal his churchgoing from wife and children. It was even said that when the Moscow Patriarchate joined the World Council of Churches at the New Delhi Assembly in 1961 the Russian delegates were only able to consult one another freely when they were in the sanctuary during the celebration of the Liturgy.

Another little understood Russian innovation on the international ecumenical scene has been the so-called 'passport speech'. Time after time Russian speakers at international meetings shock other delegates by faithfully reproducing the political views of the Kremlin. No doubt many of them do this with personal conviction. We all need to become more aware of the size of the 'beams' in our own eyes; but anyone brought up in the Soviet Union isolated for two generations from the news systems of the rest of the world, would have exceptional difficulties in identifying the facts on which objective judgements might be made. Moreover, as someone realistically observed, 'pro-government statements are the donkeys on which we travel abroad'.

There often appears to be a correlation in time between the eloquence with which a travelling churchman expounds Soviet policy abroad and the degree of pressure which is being exerted on the Churches within his country. Historians recall parallels with the behaviour of Russians under Tatar rule and of Christians in the Balkans under the Turks. Deceit may be seen as a necessary defence of the weak against their oppressors. Given the great differences in political circumstances, the desire of Western Christians to understand the situation of our fellow-Christians beyond the Iron Curtain must be accompanied by an honest recognition of the inability of 'outsiders' to see the 'whole truth' as 'insiders' see it.

Thus it is unlikely to have been a mere coincidence that the Kremlin allowed the Moscow Patriarchate to join the World Council of Churches at the very time when attacks on the Churches within the USSR were being resumed after a lull of sixteen years. Was it a mere coincidence that when Khrushchev was trying to introduce far-reaching reforms in the Soviet system, he simultaneously proclaimed that all traces of religious superstition would be eliminated from the Soviet Union by 1980? Was this move intended to placate or distract hard-line opponents of his other reforms? Only the keepers of the archives in the Kremlin could answer such questions.

Whatever the motive, a severe attack was launched against the Russian Churches in the early sixties on two fronts. Anti-religious propaganda was revived on a very large scale, and extremely effective measures of 'administrative oppression' were applied. From 1959 onwards the information office of the World Council of Churches at Geneva monitored a great

Crowds queue to visit Lenin's tomb

The Danilov bell tower under restoration

Restoring icons

Inside a prison camp

Celebration of the Liturgy in the Patriarchal cathedral

The ordination of a priest

A child receives the Sacrament

Peasant women leaving church

Religious processions in church grounds: Zagorsk (below), outside a suburban church (overleaf). Processions through the streets are forbidden.

Evangelical Christians worship in a Ukrainian forest, 1970

Baptism in a river

Inside the Baptist Evangelical church in Moscow

increase in anti-religious stories in the Soviet press. Day after day readers of Russian newspapers were being told of babies dying of pneumonia after baptism by immersion, of fanatically religious parents whose children had to be fostered, of corrupt and immoral priests, and of bishops accused of misappropriating funds or making currency deals on the black market. Confessions of apostates like A. A. Osipov (see page 82 above) were being given wide publicity.

In January 1960 a resolution of the Central Committee of the Communist Party, supported by such well-known politicians as Brezhnev, Kosygin, Suslov and Mikoyan, exhorted all trade unions, social clubs and youth organizations to revive or intensify anti-religious propaganda sessions. The teaching of atheism was reintroduced in the schools and reinforced in the Komsomol youth movement. Every high school student had to pass an examination in atheism before being admitted to a university. Hundreds of thousands of atheistic books and pamphlets were issued. Posters and leaflets publicized the statement by Yuri Gagarin, the first cosmonaut, that he had not observed God or angels in the heavens. *Science and Religion*, a serious journal of anti-religious studies, was launched with an eventual circulation of 400,000. (The maximum circulation allowed for the *Journal of the Moscow Patriarchate*, the only regular Orthodox Church publication, was 15,000.)

But the 'administrative oppression' which now began had much more serious effects. The character of the government Council for Russian Orthodox Church Affairs (CROCA) changed after the dismissal of Georgy Karpov, its chairman for sixteen years, and of his opposite number Metropolitan Nikolai. It became an instrument of supervision and oppression. In particular it compelled the church leaders themselves to take public responsibility for new measures of repression. Thus in July 1961 a synod of bishops was forced or tricked into a decision which resulted in the closure of two-thirds of the churches which had been reopened after 1943.

How was this done? The bishops were summoned to Zagorsk for the feast of St Sergius without any indication that a synod would be held. After the festal liturgy and

Gagarin poster: 'There is no God'

dinner the agenda was put before them for the first time. Three officers of the CROCA sat silently in the background while the synod met. The fourth and fatal resolution, adopted like the rest without opportunity for serious debate, concerned the organization of the parishes.

Basing himself on St Peter's saying that 'it is not right that we [the apostles] should give up preaching the word to serve tables' (Acts 6.2) the 83-year-old Patriarch Alexis said that the clergy ought to be freed from responsibility for maintaining church buildings and day-to-day administration so that they could concentrate on the celebration of the Liturgy and spiritual ministrations. They should also be removed from the risk of being accused of maladministration of church funds. Responsibility for all material aspects of parish life should therefore be given to the 'parish communities' of twenty lay members. Day-to-day business should be in the hands of executive committees elected by the parish communities and consisting of a warden, deputy warden and treasurer. These executive committees thus became in effect the employers of the parish priests, who took no part in their proceedings. The authority which parish priests derived from their bishops was taken over by executive committees which were *de facto* subordinate to the local soviets whose permission was required before meetings of the parish communities could be held. It became known later that in 1961 CROCA sent a secret circular to local soviets outlining means by which parish communities could be packed with citizens 'who would honestly carry out Soviet laws and suggestions'.

Some observers explain the acquiescence of the bishops in what proved to be such a disastrous change in the status and authority of the parish priests by citing evidence that they had been told that the only alternative was the total elimination of the visible Church. Some years later a leading churchman observed that at that time 'the string came very near to breaking'.

During the next years, thousands of churches were closed, officially at the request of the parish communities themselves. By 1980 the number open for worship had fallen from eighteen to seven thousand. (Some part of this fall in numbers might be accounted for by the massive movement of the population from the villages to the cities; but no additional churches were opened in the new urban areas.) In the same period it is estimated that the number of clergy officially employed fell from about twenty thousand to about seven thousand five hundred.

At the same time many other drastic measures were taken against the Church. The laws against giving religious instruction to minors were stretched by the issue of unpublished instructions to prevent priests giving communion to children, training servers, or encouraging boys and girls between seven and eighteen to come to church. The few surviving monasteries were cruelly hit. They were deprived of the kitchen gardens on which they depended for food, harassed by the militia, forced to pay high taxes, and saw many younger monks expelled. Organized pilgrimages were officially forbidden – though many individual pilgrims still overcame the difficulties and dangers of visiting shrines and consulting 'elders' in distant places. Many pilgrims were attacked and the newspapers spread fraudulent stories of rapes by monks. The greatly revered Pochaev monastery barely survived a prolonged series of attacks. In this period it saw the number of monks reduced from one hundred and forty-six to thirty-five.

Many parochial and monastic buildings which had survived under Stalin (though they had been closed for worship), were physically destroyed in the 1960s. Indeed, the destruction of national monuments was so great that it provoked a significant protest movement among non-believing intellectuals. Taxes of eighty per cent and more on the stipends of the clergy reduced many parishes to insolvency. Many devoted priests were deprived of their registration, or arrested for such offences as trying to attract young people to the Church, causing the death of babies by baptizing them, or recommending young men to a seminary. 'Over-zealous' bishops were removed from office on charges of immorality or fraud, or simply transferred to very distant dioceses. Strenuous efforts were made to reduce the number of baptisms by requiring the written consent of both parents and the strict registration of all baptisms in books which could be inspected by the local authorities. (Previously babies were often brought by their mothers or grandmothers and no records were kept.) Though the number of baptisms fell after 1960, in the 1970s it was still considered probable that over half the babies were being baptized, mostly without being recorded. The well-known priest Fr Dmitri Dudko affirmed that he had baptized several thousand adults during fifteen years of parochial ministry.

The eight seminaries were naturally targets for attack. Statistics are scarce, but it is probable that there were about fifteen hundred students in the fifties including those taking correspondence courses. But by 1964 five of the eight seminaries had been closed, and the number resident in the remaining three reduced to under five hundred.

Organized attempts were made to persuade individuals to give up attending services. When private persuasion failed, many men and women were publicly denounced at meetings of trade unions or social organizations. If they continued obdurate, they might be demoted or, if they were students, expelled from the university. Physical harassment of children of churchgoing parents was all too common. By a ukase of the Supreme Soviet of 19 October 1962, twenty-nine articles of the 1929 laws controlling religious practices were strengthened. For a long time the changes were not made public, but some priests and lay believers were nevertheless punished for not observing them. In some areas regulations prevented priests from celebrating the Liturgy in neighbouring parishes deprived of their priests. Other regulations were applied to prevent the churches from making a profit on the sale of candles – such profit-making being interpreted as contravening the law against 'imposing involuntary contributions'.

News of these measures spread slowly and provoked contradictory reactions inside and outside the USSR. There were some who agreed with the bishops that the Church could only survive as a visible institution if they accepted these imposed limitations and publicly denied that any 'persecution' was taking place. Some bishops, priests and layment dared to criticize the Patriarch for 'betraying the martyrs' by acquiescing in these measures. Many individuals suffered arrest, trial, imprisonment and exile for resisting the application of the new regulations. But the great majority appear to have found it expedient to bow to the storm.

There were and are an unknown number of 'crypto-Christians' including adherents of the so-called 'Catacomb Church'. In 1972 some Soviet sources estimated that there were as many as forty-eight million clandestine Christians, but this may have been a deliberately 'alarmist' figure. It is indeed probable that some of the thousands of priests deprived of their parochial appointments may have joined them. Some of these Christians would be fanatically opposed to the Patriarchal Church, but the great majority would probably still regard themselves as members of it. They might attend services at Patriarchal cathedrals and churches on major festivals, but some might deliberately refrain from seeking absolution or receiving the Sacrament from priests whom they regarded as being 'compromised'. One otherwise unconfirmed source reported that Patriarch Alexis replied to a bishop who complained that there were many 'catacomb congregations' in his diocese, by saying, 'You should thank God that there are so many courageous Christians in your diocese who have not bowed their backs to the atheists as we have done.' But it is necessary to add that there is great uncertainty about the scale of clandestine religious activities, and that some recent Russian emigrants from the USSR have said that they knew nothing of them until they came to the West.

At the time when the communist Party-State was waging this intensive anti-religious campaign, the most effective leader of the Patriarchal Church was an immensely able but also highly controversial young bishop named Nikodim Rotov. His role in the Church in the sixties compared with that of Sergius from 1927 to 1943 and of Nikolai from 1942 to 1959. Like Sergius he was gifted with 'the wisdom of serpents'. Like Nikolai he publicly supported the Soviet regime in general and the Soviet way to world peace in particular, but emphatically rejected Marxist-Leninist atheistic philosophy.

Nikodim was born in 1929. Unlike his predecessors, he had been brought up entirely under the Soviet regime. His father was an active communist and supporter of the militant anti-religious movement. He was converted and subsequently baptized as the result of a chance visit to a 'working' church. At the age of eighteen he abandoned prospects of a brilliant career as a biologist, and was tonsured as a monk by a saintly bishop who had suffered much for the faith. After service on the staff of the Russian Orthodox Mission in Jerusalem, in 1958 Nikodim joined the Patriarchal chancel-

Metropolitan Nikodim

lery in Moscow. From 1960 to 1972 he was head of the Department of External Church Relations. At the age of thirty-three he became Metropolitan of the great see of Leningrad and Ladoga. He took a prominent part in the Moscow-inspired World Christian Peace Movement and was elected a President of the World Council of Churches. In 1978 at the age of forty-nine he died of a heart-attack while on a visit to the Vatican.

Nikodim was notably charming and apparently spontaneous in personal conversations. I remember one occasion early in his career when, after a member of the WCC staff had observed that the Council could not be committed either to a *Pax Americana* or a *Pax Sovietika*, Nikodim exclaimed enthusiastically: 'Why not a *Pax Christiana*?' Years later he was talking to an American who had published a good deal of factual information about the Church in the USSR and who had criticized Nikodim's frequent public statements about 'religious freedom'. Nikodim said to him: 'Let us agree. You will continue to publish, and I will continue to deny.' On another occasion when he was challenged about telling untruths, he observed that Westerners reacted too readily to such public statements, 'but the Soviet public have got used to them'.

Leaders of Orthodox Dissent in the USSR sometimes denounced Nikodim as a wolf in sheep's clothing because he publicly denied the persecution of the Church in which he held such responsible positions. Anatoli Levitin, one of his most courageous and persistent critics, went so far as to describe him as an 'odious person' who had 'ruined the cause of the Church'. And his reforming zeal and ecumenical outlook were not popular in some more traditionalist quarters. For example, he was in favour of translating much of the Liturgy from church Slavonic into modern Russian and of healing the breach with the Roman Catholic Church. But in fact his record of achievement as a bishop was remarkable, more especially in dealing with ancient quarrels and divisions. For example he brought about at least a reconciliation between the Patriarchate and a large section of the Old Believers who had been persecuted by the Orthodox authorities for three centuries. He realized Patriarch Tikhon's hopes by securing canonical recognition of autocephalicity (i.e. independence) for the Russian Church in North America. He greatly extended the active participation of Orthodox theologians generally in the committees and staff of the World Council of Churches. He took an active part in the series of Pan-Orthodox conferences which began at Rhodes in 1961, and particularly in moves towards healing the sixteen hundred-years-old breach between the Orthodox and the 'Ancient Eastern Churches' of Egypt, Syria and India. And the most astonishing of his ecumenical achievements was the establishment of friendly relations between the Vatican and the Moscow Patriarchate with its centuries-old anti-Roman bias.

Nikodim's sermons and liturgical writings (especially of anthems for saints' days), and his manner of celebrating the Liturgy greatly impressed congregations. He is said to have persuaded large numbers of excellent candidates to seek ordination – including many mature students with good academic qualifications. He had a reputation for generosity to theological students and others in financial difficulties. He protected groups of young Christian intellectuals from attacks and is said to have provided them with foreign books. He raised the morale of his diocese by arranging unprecedented conferences of clergy and laity in Leningrad. His standing as a pastor of his diocese and ecumenical pioneer was attested by the great crowds of the faithful who attended his funeral together with an unparalleled gathering of foreign ecclesiastics, including Cardinal Willebrands from the Vatican, the Archbishop of Uppsala representing the WCC, Bishop Robert Runcie representing the Archbishop of Canterbury, and many Reformed and Lutheran churchmen.

Nikodim's meteoric career brilliantly illuminated the dilemmas and the humanly speaking irreconcilable contradictions in the life of a leading bishop in the USSR today. Bitterly denounced by some and respected as a great church leader by others, he manifested the combination of an eloquent advocate of the peace policies of the Kremlin, of a fervent Russian nationalist, and of a deeply committed Christian bishop.

Nikodim's proposals were opposed by more conservative

95

bishops including Pimen, who was elected Patriarch in 1971 after the death of Alexis at the age of ninety-two. Pimen was sixty-one. He had become a monk in 1927. There are conflicting accounts of what happened to him during the Stalin years, but in 1946 he was at a monastery in Odessa and in 1954 he became superior of the great St Sergius Lavra at Zagorsk. In 1957 he was consecrated bishop and became a permanent member of the Synod in 1961. He often humbly confesses that he lacks formal theological training; but his very conservative stand, especially on liturgical matters, seems to be popular. He publicly defends Soviet peace policies and takes the lead in conferences against nuclear arms.

At the other end of the spectrum of the Russian Orthodox Church there are those brave individual priests and laymen who dare to publish denunciations of what they regard as the 'betrayal' of the Church by the hierarchy, and who have nearly all suffered harassment, imprisonment and exile for their stand. Their record of courage and persistence against great odds deserves to be more widely known outside the USSR. It is only possible to give a very brief account of the rise and repression of 'Orthodox Dissent' in this chapter. They had some intellectual affinities with the leaders of the Russian religious renaissance in the early years of this century (see Chapter 5 above). They also had something in common with the best known Russian critic of the Soviet regime, Alexander Solzhenitsyn. But they are distinguished by the fact that they make their protest as committed Christians speaking from *within* the Patriarchal Church.

First indications of the existence of the movement became apparent in the 1960s, when, for example, Fr Vsevolod Shpiller, the highly respected archpriest of a Moscow church, publicly protested against the appointment of an unbeliever as churchwarden. In 1965 Archbishop Yermogen of Tashkent, a remarkable prelate who actually succeeded in rebuilding his cathedral, went to the Patriarchate with seven other bishops to protest against the closure of churches and other evil effects of the fatal decision of the Synod in 1961. Yermogen was removed from his diocese, but two Moscow priests, Nikolai Eshliman and Gleb Yakunin, began writing

Gleb Yakunin

letters to the Patriarch in which they pointed out the many
ways in which the government's Council for the Affairs of
the Orthodox Church was contravening the laws of the
Soviet Union on the separation of Church and state. They
accused the Patriarchate of conniving with the Soviet authorities and thereby 'violating the apostolic command by
compromising with the world'. In December 1965 the two
priests went further and wrote an open letter to the Head of

State and sent copies to the Patriarch, the other bishops and abroad. This kind of action obviously went beyond the limits of what was permissible in the Soviet Union, and the Patriarch forbade the priests to continue to exercise their clerical functions.

They were not, however, silenced, and in 1975 Fr Yakunin and a young layman named Lev Regelson managed to send a strong appeal to the delegates of the fifth Assembly of the World Council of Churches meeting at Nairobi. They told how the Church was suffering, although the Patriarchate continued to deny that persecution was taking place. They regretted that the Council had failed to give sufficient attention to religious persecution, but they hoped that 'a feeling of genuine Christian solidarity' would emerge. They asked for support from the Council for an eight-point programme of publicity for the sufferers, for prayer, for personal contacts and letters, for protests to the Soviet authorities, for aid for Christians who wished to emigrate, and for more Bibles. The appeal was remarkable for its restraint. They did not, for example, call for the Assembly to denounce the Patriarchate or to expel the Russian Church from the WCC.

Their appeal received considerable unofficial publicity and eventually provoked a long debate in full Assembly under the heading of the observance of the Helsinki agreements on human rights and religious freedom. Eventually a resolution was agreed which did not name the USSR specifically but called upon the General Secretary to consult with the Churches in all the states that had signed the Helsinki agreements. The two dissenters had secured a notable success in bringing the issue to open discussion by the Assembly – and the Patriarchate had not been forced by its Soviet government mentors to withdraw from the Council. In the following year they set up a 'Christian Committee for the Defence of Believers' Rights in the USSR', which was for a time able to compile and transmit abroad a remarkable number of useful documents. But in 1979 Fr Yakunin was arrested and the Christian Committee ceased to be a productive source of information.

Another prolific Orthodox apologist, Boris Talentov, died

Patriarch Pimen

in prison in 1971, and yet another, Anatoli Levitin, was imprisoned and then emigrated on his release. Alexander Ogorodnikov, who had set up a religio-philosophical seminar in Moscow, was imprisoned in 1973 together with other members of the group whose names became known through Amnesty International. So by 1980 most of the leaders of the movement of Orthodox Dissent, who had spoken out so

99

boldly both to the Orthodox Church leaders and to ecumenical organizations outside Russia, had been silenced. Nevertheless other correspondents successfully stimulated further discussion of issues of religious liberty both on the floor and in the corridors of the sixth WCC Assembly at Vancouver in 1983 – discussions in which the Archbishop of Canterbury took part.

Journalists outside Russia tend to concentrate attention on the politics of the Patriarchate and the protests of dissenters, but it is exceedingly difficult to discover how far these concerns are shared by the many millions of faithful Christians who make up the congregations in the churches open for worship in the USSR. Direct information is only available about a very small number of the parochial clergy. It is likely that the majority try to carry out their liturgical and pastoral responsibilities without involving themselves in ecclesiastical or national politics. However, the story of one well-known parish priest illuminates the changing conditions under which many others are working who are unknown to the outside world.

Fr Dmitri Dudko served in the Red Army during the war and afterwards spent eight and a half years in a penal labour camp – the charge is not known for certain. He became a Christian in the camp. He was ordained in 1960 at the age of thirty-eight and became a parish priest in Moscow in 1962. He soon became known for his preaching and effectiveness as a spiritual counsellor. He spoke openly of subjects which were not normally mentioned: for example, the relation between drunkenness, hooliganism and crime with atheism, or the presence in the congregation 'of some who are sent here on purpose by someone else'. After eleven years of faithful ministry he announced that on Saturday evenings he would answer written questions on the content of the faith. The public response was extraordinary. He spoke clearly and forcibly on a variety of aspects of morality and belief. He did not criticize the Soviet regime as such. When questioners attacked the Patriarch, he spoke sympathetically of his situation, saying, 'Who has fewer civil rights than the Patriarch? They say he is surrounded by thousands of informers. Everything he does against his conscience he does under pressure, and of course, out of weakness, like any man . . .'

Inevitably, three months after these Saturday evening sessions began, the church authorities were pressurized into transferring him out of Moscow to a village fifty miles away, while the Soviet press accused him of attacking the government and of immoral relationships. But numbers of people made the long journey out to hear him preach, and after a few months he was dismissed from this charge also, although his parishioners protested. By this time his case had become known abroad in the World Council of Churches and other circles, and this may account for the fact that he was not arrested but simply transferred to another country parish. There he suffered much harassment, but worked on quietly for several years during which he was even able to take the unprecedented step of publishing a parish magazine. However, in January 1980 he was arrested and charged with 'anti-Soviet agitation and propaganda'. Immediately many protests were made both to the civil authorities and to the Patriarch on the ground that he had only worked openly and legally in his parish without any political involvement. Orthodox bishops in the West belonging to the Moscow jurisdiction (such as Metropolitan Anthony of Sourozh in London) joined in the protests.

After spending five months in prison without being brought to trial, Fr Dudko unexpectedly appeared on Soviet television and publicly confessed his failure to follow Patriarchal policy towards the state. The Soviet press represented him as having been the dupe of Western politicians. Russian believers and foreign commentators did not know what to make of this statement. Was it formulated by the secret police? Was it extorted by force or under drugs? Had an expert interrogator been able to persuade him that to make this confession was an honourable way of being able to continue his priestly ministry and avoid another long period of imprisonment or exile? Fr Dudko's later statements about it were confused and unenlightening. It is noteworthy that after his release without trial his bishop, Metropolitan Yuvenaly, one of the inner circle of the Patriarchate, put him in charge of another parish and came specially to celebrate the

Liturgy with him. Many of his 'spiritual children' are said to have deserted him, but he seems to have been allowed to carry on with his pastoral ministry unimpeded.

Evidence concerning the situation since the rise of Gorbachev is inconclusive. On one side are only very limited indications that *glasnost* might include some amelioration of the restrictive laws concerning the Churches. (An official account of the present legal situation is printed as Appendix 2. Like all similar documents it should be read with caution, but it indicates the legal grounds on which defenders of the rights of registered congregations can sometimes appeal successfully against arbitrary acts by Soviet officials.)

On the other side it seems that during the last five years the regulations concerning religious societies have quite often been administered with less severity. The case of the theological students may perhaps indicate what may happen more generally. In 1961 the number of seminaries was reduced from eight to three (see page 9), but in 1987 there were said to be more seminarians than there were twenty-five years ago. How has this come about? Zagorsk has trebled its intake by packing the students in 'like herrings in a box'. Leningrad has doubled its capacity by regaining the use of a previously alienated building. At Odessa, the Rector, who was described as 'a very clever administrator', obtained permission to restore the old and cramped seminary building. But it 'fell down' – and was then rebuilt with double the accommodation. Government officials accepted the *fait accompli*. Both Church and state authorities have their own reasons for keeping dark about the number of theological students, but it seems reasonable to conclude that in recent years the total (including those taking correspondence courses) has risen from under a thousand to well over two thousand.

What about the congregations? Always bearing in mind that the number of churches open for worship is very small (under fifty for a population of nine million in Moscow), the number of worshippers at any one service is very high. City churches are full twice or thrice daily. Soviet sources themselves estimate that churchgoers number about thirty million or one-sixth of the population of European Russia. A recent visitor to a Sunday service at the Patriarchal Cathedral in Moscow reported that it was full to the doors; that women outnumbered men by five to one; that about one-third of the women were not the famous *babushkas* ('grannies') but young mothers with children; that about one-third of the men were also between sixteen and twenty-five; but that there were very few middle-aged men or women.

But recent developments seem to indicate some reduction of the pressures on the Churches. The first is the return to the Church of the Danilov monastery which was founded by Prince Daniel (see page 11 above) in the thirteenth century, but which had been used as a penitentiary for hooligans for many years after 1917. The Church has been allowed facilities for the restoration of the walls, bell-tower, three churches and monastic buildings. It has already built accommodation for the monks, and a handsome office for the Department of Foreign Church Relations. It is engaged in building a residence for the Patriarch, a large ecumenical centre and a hostel for foreign visitors. The cost will amount to many millions which will all come from the offerings of the faithful.

The second surprising and hopeful development in the last three years is the permission given to the Church to mount large-scale national and international celebrations of the Millennium of the 'Baptism of Rus' in AD 988. An elaborate programme for the Jubilee Year has already been published. Intourist is arranging many special tours for pilgrims from abroad. The Church's publications department has been authorized to produce many special publications. And the Church has been able to open a factory in the vicinity of Moscow for the production of souvenirs and church furnishings of many kinds.

In April 1987 it was announced that forty-two prisoners of conscience had been released before completing their sentences. They included Alexander Ogorodnikov, animator of the religio-philosophical seminar at Moscow, and Father Gleb Yakunin, who was soon reinstated as a priest by decision of the Synod, and appointed by Metropolitan

Yuvenaly as the priest of a church in a small town twenty-four miles from Moscow.

What can have motivated the Kremlin to make these concessions? There is no direct evidence; but as in Stalin's case forty-five years ago, certain surmises can be made. The Kremlin may consider that some relaxations of the treatment of individual Christians whose cases have been known outside the USSR may add verisimilitude to speeches about *glasnost* and *détente*. The Millennium can be treated as a national festival without great spiritual significance. Now that the Church has established such extensive international relations, a refusal to allow the celebration of such an important anniversary might affect public responses in Western countries to Mr Gorbachev's peace proposals. In any case increased numbers of foreign visitors will bring in quantities of much needed foreign currency.

But whatever the motives of the Soviet authorities in granting these facilities, there is no doubt that the Patriarchate will have the enthusiastic support of millions of the faithful in celebrating this crucial event in the history of the Russian Church and nation. In 1940, twenty-three years after the Revolution, few outsiders would have predicted that the Church would successfully survive for seventy years under a communist dictatorship dedicated to the elimination of religion. It is true that church life is still severely restricted, and that church leaders have to walk an extremely narrow path between the pressures of the state authorities and the expectations of the faithful, but no one can doubt the spiritual vitality of the millions who come to worship, or the confidence with which, after overcoming so many trials, they look forward to the future. The Phoenix has indeed risen from the ashes.

10
The Witness of the Nonconformists
1929–1988

The oldest and still one of the largest nonconformist Churches in the USSR is that of the Old Believers. They are divided among several 'jurisdictions' and statistical information about them is very scarce. But students believe that there are probably more than a million. Thanks partly to the efforts of Metropolitan Nikodim, in 1971 the Patriarchal Church lifted the decrees of excommunication pronounced against them in the seventeenth century. But it is difficult to discover whether this gesture has made any difference to their way of life or relationships. Most observers seem to agree that the various groupings of Old Believers go on quietly in their conservative ways much as before without paying attention to other Churches. They tend to be very suspicious of outsiders, but foreigners who have been able to attend their services report that the atmosphere of medieval Orthodoxy has been preserved in an astonishing way, and that they still possess some superb icons.

There are other dissenting Orthodox groups about which even less is known. Possibly the largest consists of the 'True Orthodox', who went underground in the 1930s because they opposed Metropolitan Sergius's policy of seeking an accommodation with the Soviet state. They are extremely secretive – and have good reason for being so. Some students consider that they also might number as many as a million.

But the most numerous group of nonconformists consists of Baptist and Evangelical congregations. For a brief period after 1917 they had benefited by deliverance from harsh Tsarist–Orthodox pressures while the anti-religious activities of the Soviet state were concentrated against the Orthodox Church. But from 1929 onwards the severe Soviet anti-religious laws were enforced against Baptists and Orthodox alike. Most of the Baptist leaders were imprisoned or silenced, and their national organization ceased to function for the next fourteen years. Unlike the Orthodox they did not have even that degree of protection which was derived from long association with Russian nationalism.

Locally, Stalin's savage campaign for the collectivization of agriculture, the elimination of the kulaks, and the suppression of Ukrainian separatism, destroyed numerous Evangelical congregations. The industry, honesty and abstention from heavy drinking of many Evangelicals had raised them above the economic level of the majority of the peasants; consequently they suffered disproportionately when the Party encouraged the seizure of cattle, farm machinery and homes for the benefit of the new collective farms.

The smaller Mennonite congregations suffered even more severely. Their non-Russian origin, their pacifism, and their continuing links with co-religionists outside the USSR, made them specially vulnerable. The final blow came with the German invasion, when they and other German-speaking peoples in the Ukraine were forcibly evacuated to Siberia for fear lest they should collaborate with the invaders. In fact, contrary to the government's expectations, most Protestant Christians in unoccupied Russia proved to be as patriotic and supportive of the national resistance as their Orthodox brethren. Later they benefited equally from the relaxation of anti-religious activities.

In 1944 Yakob Zhidkov, a very 'patriarchal' figure, with a long white beard, emerged as president, and A. V. Karev as treasurer, of a new 'All-Union Council of Evangelical Christians and Baptists' (AUCECB). Many Pentecostalists joined the Council in 1945 as a means of securing legal recognition, and the remnant of the Mennonites followed them in 1963. So for a brief period the vision of Protestant unity which had attracted so many leaders since the 1880s was realized.

Nevertheless below the surface there were serious tensions. Some were doctrinal, for example, over baptism; but these were settled. Most concerned the relations of the AUCECB with the Soviet state. Many Protestants had suffered severely from repression both before 1917 and after 1929. Many were heirs of the tradition of independency, according to which the state had no right to interfere with the inner life of Christian congregations. Although the leaders of the AUCECB had been imprisoned under Stalin they were suspected of having made some kind of secret deal with the state authorities before they were given permission to operate publicly. The strong congregationalist tradition of the Baptists also led them to reject any kind of centralized ecclesiastical authority. Others objected that the Council was a self-appointed body not subject to the control of a democratically elected congress of representatives of the local churches, and that through the designation of regional 'senior presbyters' it was exercising undue influence over local relations with state officials, the registration of congregations and the official recognition of ministers. With so many causes of disagreement it was not surprising that the unity of the 'Union' came under strain.

As the years passed many more congregations sought and gained legal status through registration, but they resented the efforts of the AUCECB to keep their activities within the very strict limits imposed by Soviet law. They did however benefit by the quiet disregard by many local authorities of many of the harsh measures that had previously been enforced. By 1959 many more 'prayer-houses' had been opened. More pastors had been appointed. Many choirs had been trained, some including a high proportion of young people. Several limited editions of the Bible had been printed or imported. Books of hymns and devotional songs had been published. Contacts had been resumed with the Baptist World Alliance. A small number of students, including Yakob Zhidkov's son Michael, had been allowed to go abroad to study theology. These were substantial gains; but they were precarious because the basic anti-religious laws still remained; congregations were subject to the caprice of local officials; the press and radio continued to publish malicious reports about believers, and local communist zealots could easily stir up trouble for congregations.

In 1959 Khrushchev's relaunched anti-religious campaign hit the Baptist-Evangelical 'establishment' like a tornado. The leaders were put under intense pressure. In 1960 they issued an Instruction to senior presbyters which was so negative and so contrary to the spiritual traditions of the

Baptist-Evangelical Churches that it led to widespread revolt against the Council. (It was in fact the Baptist equivalent of the decrees of the contemporary synod of the Orthodox Church; see page 87 above.)

The Instruction stated that many activities, expressly forbidden by the law of 1929 and subsequent revisions, were being carried on and must now stop. Boys and girls under eighteen had been baptized. Church funds had been used to give charitable assistance to the families of prisoners and others. Bible evenings and other special meetings had been organized without permission from the state authorities. Excursions had been arranged for young people. There had been unauthorized meetings for preachers and choir leaders. The senior presbyters were told to insist on the strict observance of the law limiting church activities to worship, to end the chase after new believers, to reduce baptisms of people between eighteen and thirty 'to an absolute minimum', and to prevent children from attending services. (This was not in fact forbidden by the law.) One member of the All-Union Council went so far as to affirm that the 'chief goal of religious services at the present time is not to attract new members but to satisfy the spiritual needs of believers'. (The phrase translated 'at the present time' may have been specially significant.)

It is easy to understand the shock experienced by congregations and their pastors when they heard what the leaders of the All-Union Council were saying to them. It appeared to condemn many of the *de facto* concessions made to the Churches since 1943 and to be evidence that the Council itself was collaborating with the Soviet authorities in the destruction of church life by dismissing 'over-zealous pastors', restricting church activities and dissolving congregations.

In this crisis three pastors formed an 'Action Group'. They were Alexei Prokoviev (who had been imprisoned 1941–51 and again in 1954), Georgi Vins (whose father had died in a prison-camp in 1929) and Gennadi Krychkov. In August 1961 they addressed a letter 'to all registered and unregistered congregations', in which they affirmed that 'in our days Satan is dictating to the AUCECB decisions which directly contradict the commands of God. The leaders of the All-Union Council have caused a split in our congregations.'

In February 1962 the Action Group met secretly and transformed itself into an 'Organizing Committee'. Six months later they excommunicated the officers of the AUCECB and twenty of the senior presbyters. They demanded that permission should be given for the organization of a democratically elected Congress which could call the All-Union Council to account.

At the same time pressure from the Soviet side was somewhat relaxed. An article in the anti-religious journal *Science and Religion* admitted that 'rough treatment and administrative pressure had been responsible for producing schism in the Church'. A later article said that 'a schism may weaken the Church, but it can lead to a revitalization of religion and a stronger growth in church life and activities. Therefore a schism does not serve the interests of Soviet society.' (In other words, schism made the All-Union Council less effective as an instrument for controlling the congregations.) A little later the Communist Youth paper *Komsonolskaya Pravda* noted that 'the closing of churches does not make atheists of believers. On the contrary it attracts people to religion and embitters their hearts. Brutality to believers arouses sympathy from the public.' It was indeed obvious that a rapid increase in the number of 'underground' congregations would be unacceptable to the government.

So in October 1963 the All-Union Council was itself allowed to organize a national congress. It was attended by two hundred and fifty delegates, but supporters of the Action Group (now usually referred to as the *Initsiativniki*) did not attend, and many of their leaders were already in prison. The Congress repealed the 1960 Statute and Instruction. It adopted a much more democratic constitution under which the All-Union Council would be elected by a Congress meeting every three years. The right of all church members to preach was reaffirmed. The Instructions forbidding the attendance of boys and girls at services, contacts with 'unregistered' congregations, and holding services in homes, were quietly dropped. At another larger Congress of 450 held in 1966 other demands made by the *Initsiativniki*

Lydia Vins

were implemented. A few days before he died, Yakob Zhidkov himself asked the Congress to forgive him for signing the 1960 Instruction. The independence of local congregations was affirmed. Senior presbyters were no longer to be nominated by the All-Union Council but elected by regional conferences of presbyters. (There is a parallel in the procedures for the appointment of rural deans in the Church of England in modern times). So the steadfast witness of the Baptist Reformers, and especially of women members, finally enabled the All-Union Council to adopt many of their proposals. As Walter Sawatsky wrote: 'The cautious Moscow leadership retreated gracefully and with secret pleasure' from the oppressive stance they had been forced to adopt in 1961.

But in spite of the reforms introduced by the All-Union Council the *Initsiativniki* were not satisfied. They formed their own Council of Evangelical Christians and Baptists (CCECB). For some years members of the All-Union Council made attempts to persuade individuals and congregations to rejoin them. At first the best that they could claim was that the movement away into the ranks of the dissidents had ceased; but in the last ten years it seems that the number of congregations which are both registered with the authorities and affiliated to the AUCECB has increased considerably. Probably this indicates that many congregations had been classed as 'unregistered', not because they objected to registration in principle, but because local Soviet authorities constantly postponed consideration of their applications for registration. In recent years an unknown number of congregations have taken advantage of a new possibility offered by the Soviet Council of Religious Affairs. Under this arrangement they could be legally registered without being compelled to acknowledge the authority of the All-Union Council. On the other hand the Soviet Council for Religious Affairs itself has now taken responsibility for registration away from local authorities, and is reported to have made a large number of apparently quite arbitrary negative decisions.

Pressures on all Protestants, and especially on members of unregistered congregations, are often very severe. Reports continue to appear in the Soviet press or in underground publications of believers being harassed in various ways. Private houses used for prayer-meetings have been pulled down; pastors have been deprived of residence permits; parents have lost their jobs and have then been deported or imprisoned as 'parasites'; children have suffered from discrimination and organized bullying at school and have been removed from their homes. The number of pastors and members in prison or penal work-camps fluctuates around three hundred. The outside world has been kept informed of their fate by a remarkable underground organization known as the Council for Prisoners' Relatives (CPR), in which Georgi Vins' widowed mother Lydia took a leading part, for which she was imprisoned. Since 1964 the CPR have collected and periodically circulated lists of Baptists and Evangelicals imprisoned for their faith. Often they have been able also to publish details of their trials. Copies have been regularly sent abroad and organizations such as Amnesty International and Keston College have reproduced them. The attitude of the leaders of the CPR to those responsible for the persecutions they record has been truly 'evangelical'. They exhort their readers 'not to tolerate resentful feelings towards their oppressors but to pray for those who slander and oppress them'. They have even been able to collect and distribute shoes and clothing for the children of parents in prison. This is an illegal activity for a religious organization in the USSR, but it seems that in many places it has gone on unobserved or unpunished.

The fate of Georgi Vins himself was typical of many other Reformed Baptists less known outside the USSR. After his arrest in May 1966 he was held in prison for five months until his trial in November. He was actually charged with circulating literature in defiance of the laws concerning religious cults. The court-room was packed with partisans of the state Council for Religious Affairs, and Vins' family and friends were excluded. The court sat for no less than fourteen hours on the first day and fifteen hours on the second. Finally he was sentenced to three years in a 'special regime' (i.e. specially severe) penal work-camp. After his release he applied for permission to serve as a full-time secretary for the CCECB. When permission was not unexpectedly refused, he went 'underground' and succeeded in evading detection for four years. In 1974 he was again arrested, tried and sentenced to five years in a labour camp to be followed by five years of internal exile; but in 1979 he was exchanged for a Soviet spy, and went with his mother to the United States, where she died.

The Vins family were expelled from the Soviet Union, but other dissident families and groups, especially Pentecostalists, suffered because their applications for permission to emigrate were refused. One such group became known world-wide as the 'Siberian Seven' because for many months they took political asylum in the cellars of the American Embassy. More recently reports have emerged of the trials of a larger group of would-be emigrants who since 1983 have been labelled the 'Siberian Seventy'. For two years they had been harassed, fined and imprisoned for persistently meeting for worship although they had not been 'registered' by the authorities. As a number of them had relatives outside the USSR, they decided to emigrate as a group. They notified the authorities of their intention and handed over their internal passports. When their request was refused some of the men repeatedly organized hunger-strikes. They posted large notices outside their houses explaining the reason for their protests. The authorities replied by an intensive propaganda campaign, sacking offenders from their jobs and harassing their children. In 1984 eight of the protesters were arrested, tried and sentenced to three or five years in penal labour-camps. Reports in April 1987 said that one family had been granted emigration visas, but that the rest were still under severe pressure. They asked for prayers and publicity in the West.

Far too many similar reports are received, not only about Christians but also about large numbers of Jewish would-be emigrants (the so-called 'refuseniks'). Such denials of elementary human rights are always grievous and the victims deserve our practical support and our prayers; but they are a minority. Misunderstandings are compounded when exaggerated accounts of the situation are published. When, for example, Richard Wurmbrand and others claim that 'tens of thousands' of Russian Christians are being imprisoned for their faith, it is necessary to check the alleged facts with information from other sources. Wurmbrand compares the fate of faithful Christians in the Soviet Union today with that of the martyrs of the first centuries AD. He believes that Communism is the supreme embodiment of evil (going in this respect far beyond the position of most of the Reformed Baptists in Russia), and he condemns as traitors to the faith church leaders who come to any 'accommodation' with the Soviet authorities. He expects that the faithful witness of the underground Church will destroy the Soviet Union from within.

To keep the known facts in perspective it is necessary to recall that there are at least thirty million Orthodox Christians in the USSR who openly profess their faith by church attendance and in other ways. There are at least three million Baptist-Evangelicals, Mennonites and Pentecostalists who do likewise. All these accept registration by the state and keep the public expression and practice of their faith more or less within the limits imposed by Soviet laws. The number of Reformed Baptists and others who conscientiously reject any relationship with the Soviet state is probably about three hundred thousand – that is about three per cent of the total. The number of those condemned to prison or work-camps under the anti-religious laws is about three hundred at any one time.

Christians as such do not have an easy time in the USSR. The law restricts public religious activities to worship in state registered congregations. The press and television frequently publicize the alleged misdeeds of believers. Congregations and individuals live under threat of hostile actions by local officials or party zealots. Church leaders are constantly compelled to agree to painful compromises in order that their Churches may continue to have any kind of public existence even under the harsh conditions imposed by the state. Occasionally the pressures are somewhat relaxed, as in the case of the return of the Danilov monastery to the Orthodox Church in 1983, the authorization in July 1987 of the import of one hundred thousand Bibles and five thousand sets of William Barclay's New Testament commentaries in Russian, for the use of Baptist-Evangelicals, and the permission given for the Orthodox to print another one hundred thousand Bibles as part of the celebration of the millennium of the 'Baptism of Rus' in 1988.

But whether political pressures on the Russian Churches temporarily increase or diminish Christians in the USSR deserve and value the prayers of their fellow-Christians throughout the world. Even if the political stance of some of the Protestant martyrs and the claims made on their behalf by others may not be universally accepted, Christians outside Russia can thank God for the faithfulness of their witness and continue to pray for their deliverance from evil.

11
The Significance of the Russian Experience

In 1917 Lenin was confident that the Russian Church, deprived of support by the state, would die out with the deaths of the 'grandmothers' who formed the majority in the congregations. In 1929 Stalin gave this 'inevitable' historical process a powerful push by codifying anti-religious laws, drastically enforcing them, and mounting a nation-wide propaganda campaign. In 1959 Khrushchev declared that all unscientific superstition should be eliminated from the Soviet Union by 1980.

But these confident predictions have not been fulfilled. Today at least six thousand Orthodox churches are open for worship, and hundreds of Baptist congregations are officially 'registered' with the authorities. In towns and cities the churches, though small in numbers compared with the population, are crowded with worshippers more than once a day seven days a week. The proportion of ethnic Russians who openly attend services in the USSR is higher than the proportion of worshippers to population in Western Europe and Britain. At major festivals enormous crowds gather round the larger churches. The central Baptist church in Moscow is attended by over ten thousand worshippers a week.

These figures are supported by other observations. Though for good reason records of baptisms are seldom available, it is reasonable to assume that the majority of the population of European Russia have been baptized. Congregations today include many more young people than twenty years ago. There are more candidates for training for the ministry than there are places. There is a great demand for memorial services for the dead – even if this only means that their names are included in long lists read out in services. In many cemeteries recent graves marked with crosses greatly outnumber those marked with red stars.

Many committed Christians are not included in any statistics either because they live far away from any 'working' church, or because they are confined in penal camps or prisons, or have good family reasons for not attending a church. Nevertheless they pray and live by faith. Evidence keeps coming in of the existence of a wide circle of 'crypto-Christians'. Stalin's daughter Svetlana Alliluyeva was baptized secretly as an adult while she was still living in the Kremlin. Some sober estimates put the number of committed Christians in the USSR at over fifty million. The majority of them will have been taught atheism at school.

1988 sees the paradoxical spectacle of an aggressively atheist regime facilitating the celebration by the Churches of the Millennium of the 'Baptism of Rus'. Seventy years after the Communist Revolution the Churches have not only survived severe legal restrictions, aggressive atheist propaganda and the death or imprisonment of thousands of martyrs: the Phoenix has repeatedly risen from the ashes. How, under God, can we account for this remarkable record of Christian life and witness in such hostile circumstances for so many years?

Some suggest that there is a peculiar religious streak in the psychological make-up of the Slavs; but congregations are much smaller in Bulgarian and Serbian Orthodox churches than in the USSR. Others point to the peculiarly close relationship between the Russian Church and nation. It is indeed true that the Church played a large part in the unification of the Russian tribes and rival princedoms, in maintaining morale during the centuries of Tatar domination, in consolidating a central government, and in rallying national resistance to Teutonic, Swedish, Polish, Lithuanian, French, British and Nazi German invaders. Soviet historians themselves acknowledge the important role of the Church in the development of the Russian state and Russian art in the past; but they still consider that religion should have no place in the future. However, evidence of the vestigial influence of the Christian past can still emerge in the most unexpected quarters. For example, while Brezhnev

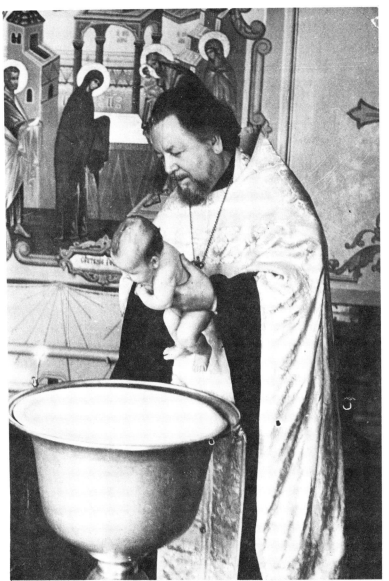

The baptism of a Russian child

was still in power, two religious leaders were presented to him at a reception. They expected only a formal greeting; but Brezhnev astonished them by putting his arms round their shoulders and saying: 'I've terrible things on my mind. These Americans and the bomb! Pray for me! Pray for me!' Perhaps an inheritance from peasant forefathers lies behind such remarks.

Even so, the close association of the Church with Russian nationalism does not explain the steadfastness in the faith of so many individual believers in the face of such powerful anti-religious pressures. So a sociological explanation has been offered. This focuses on the traditional 'icon-corner' in Orthodox homes and on the corresponding Protestant emphasis on families praying together. Thus, though many thousands of churches and 'prayer-houses' are no longer open for worship, family worship can and does continue, aided by the many priests and pastors who have been forced to go 'underground'. Consequently the removal, imprisonment or (in early years) execution of thousands of clergy did not have such a catastrophic effect in Russia as it might have done in Churches which depend more heavily on the ministrations of their clergy. Against this there is evidence that some leading Russian churchmen were brought up in completely atheistic families.

Russian Christians themselves often compare their situation with that of Christians in the Roman Empire before Constantine issued his Edict of Toleration. The point of the comparison is not only that in both epochs the Church was a persecuted minority, but also that Christians were sustained in their times of trial by confidence in the final victory of God. The faith of Christians in contemporary Russia and in the Roman Empire embraces the double hope of personal resurrection after death and of the coming of God's Kingdom in this world.

So in a conference on nuclear disarmament between a delegation of Russian churchmen and English church leaders in 1983, Metropolitan Anthony of Sourozh, the well-known religious broadcaster and writer who represents the Moscow Patriarchate in London, drew attention to the relevance of some passages in the New Testament which

Western Christians tend to disregard. He referred to such sayings as: 'When you hear of wars and rumours of wars, do not be alarmed ... In those days after that tribulation you will see the Son of Man coming in the clouds with great power and glory' (Mark 13.7, 26), and 'Be faithful unto death and I will give you the crown of life' (Revelation 2.10). Moreover there is a strain of Russian spirituality which is nourished by the belief that God in Christ humiliated himself to share the bitter pains of human injustice, torture, degradation and death, and that Christ's resurrection revealed that this sharing was and is a basic aspect of God's true glory. Many Russian Christians must have been supported by such insights in their trials.

For Orthodox believers especially, participation in celebrations of the Holy Liturgy lies at the very heart of their endurance in the faith. The Soviets probably permitted the Churches to continue with this one activity because from the materialist point of view it is completely useless. Perhaps with their secularist presuppositions they forgot that during the long centuries of Turkish rule in south-east Europe it was the Holy Liturgy which kept the Church alive. Many Christians would agree with the affirmation of Metropolitan Alexis Simansky, later elected Patriarch, that the celebration of the Liturgy was the only essential function of the Church Militant here on earth (see page 81 above).

Many visitors can testify that attendence at a celebration of the Holy Liturgy in a Russian church is a dramatic, emotional experience of a 'world' very different indeed from everyday life in the Soviet Union. The celebrations may be over-long, liturgically unreformed, and highly repetitive, but surrounded by the icons of the saints and by congregations often numbering many hundreds standing packed closely together, the worshipper senses the immense power of the Orthodox tradition to convey the sacramental presence of God. All are linked together in corporate worship as they join in singing the Creed and the Lord's Prayer and familiar responses, listen to the choirs singing the anthems of the day, and share in the litanies for 'the peace of the whole world and the union of all', 'for deliverance from all tribulation, wrath and necessity', 'for pardon and remission of our sins and transgressions' and 'for a Christian ending for our lives, painless, blameless and peaceful, and a sure defence before the dread judgement seat of Christ'.

Historical memories, associations of patriotism, family worship, Christian hope, the transcendent worship of the Holy Liturgy – all these may contribute to the phoenix-like resurrections of the Russian Church from the destructive fires of an atheistic revolution. It is not for mortals to know the whole secret of the resistance and renaissance of the faithful in the USSR. But those who belong to other Christian traditions can thank God for the survival of visible Churches in Russia against all the expectations of the secularists, and more especially for the courage and devotion shown by so many millions of our Russian fellow-Christians, both Orthodox and Protestant.

Can we go further? Is it possible for Christians living in other cultures and under non-communist regimes to learn from the Russian experience? It is not easy to answer this question. Too many Western Christians are totally ignorant of what has happened in and to the Churches in the USSR during the seventy years of Soviet rule. Among those who do know something many seem to be most moved by sympathy for those who are suffering persecution. Others have over-romantic pictures of a few 'heroes of the faith'. Is then the story of Russian Christianity interesting and even at times inspiring, but with little direct relevance to the witness of Christians who live outside the borders of the Communist Empire?

Archpriest Vitaly Borovoi, the wise and spiritually gifted priest who headed the Moscow Patriarchate's delegation at Geneva for many years, has more than once called upon members of other Churches to recognize that Russian Christians have become the Church's 'experts' on living in a hostile secular environment. He implied that the Russian experience could have a direct bearing on the future of other Churches because Western countries too are rapidly losing any grounds for being regarded as being 'Christian'. Similar waves of godless secularism are washing away the foundations of supposedly 'religious' cultures in other continents also. As the dark clouds of secularism and unbelief roll round the world, it may become apparent that much more serious study needs to be done of ways in which the sufferings and the triumphs of Christians in the USSR are becoming more and more relevant to the life and witness of Churches in other parts of the world.

One hundred years hence church historians may well consider the endurance and witness to the Resurrection faith of Russian Christians as being one of the most heartening and significant developments of the twentieth century.

Bibliography

Main sources and suggestions for further reading:

PART ONE
General
Pares, B., *History of Russia*. Jonathan Cape 1949, 1955.
Lawrence, J., *Russia in the Making*. Allen & Unwin 1957.
Kochan, L., and Abraham, A., *The Making of Modern Russia* (2nd edn). Penguin 1983.

Church History and Doctrine
Arseniev, N., *Russian Piety* (1964).
Arseniev, N., *The Russian Orthodox Church* (Moscow Patriarchate. Central Books 1982).
Bulgakov, S., *The Orthodox Church*. Geoffrey Bles 1935.
French, R. M., *The Eastern Orthodox Church*. Hutchinson 1951.
Frere, W., *Links in the Chain of Russian Church History* (1913).
Lossky, V., *Mystical Theology of the Eastern Church*. J. Clarke 1957.
Schmemann, A., *The Historical Road of Eastern Orthodoxy*. Harvill 1965.
Stanley, A. P., *The Eastern Church*. John Murray 1861.
Zernov, N., *The Church of the Eastern Christians*. SPCK 1942.
Zernov, N., *The Russians and Their Church*. SPCK 1945.

Chapters One, Two and Three
Fedotov, G. P., *A Treasure of Russian Spirituality*. Sheed & Ward 1950.
Zernov, N., *Moscow, the Third Rome* (2nd edn). SPCK 1938.
Zernov, N., *St Sergius: the Builder of Russia*. SPCK 1939.

Chapter Four
Arseniev, N., *Holy Moscow*. SPCK 1940.
Bateman, A. F. Dobbie, tr., *St Serafim of Sarov*. SPCK 1936.
Creighton, M., *Life and Letters*. Longmans, Green and Co. 1904.
French, R. M., tr., *The Way of a Pilgrim*. SPCK 1930, 1986.
French, R. M., tr., *The Pilgrim Continues his Way*. SPCK 1943, 1986.
Gorodetsky, N., *The Humiliated Christ in Modern Russian Thought*. (1938).
Gorodetsky, N., *St Tikhon Zadonsky*. SPCK 1951.
Graham, S., *The Way of Martha and the Way of Mary*. Macmillan 1916.
Zander, L., *Dostoevsky*. Haskell 1974.
Zander, V. *St Serafim of Sarov*. The Fellowship of St Alban and St Sergius 1968.

Zernov, N., *The Russian Religious Renaissance in the 20th Century*. Darton, Longman & Todd 1963.

Chapter Six
Avvakum, 'The Life of Archpriest Avvakum by Himself', in Fedotov, G. P., op.cit. sup.
Brandenburg, H., *The Meek and the Mighty*. Mowbray 1976.

PART TWO
Chapter Seven
Anderson, P. B., *People, Church and State in Modern Russia*. SCM Press 1944.
Beeson, T., *Discretion and Valour: Religious Conditions in Russia and Eastern Europe* (2nd edn). Fount 1982.
Fedotov, G. P., *The Russian Church since the Revolution*. SPCK 1928.
Fletcher, W. C., *Nikolai* (1968).
Fletcher, W. C., *The Russian Orthodox Church Underground, 1917–70*. Oxford University Press 1971.
Hecker, J., *Religion under the Soviets* (1927). (Communist view)
Kolarz, W., *Religion in the Soviet Union*. Macmillan 1961.
Lawrence, J., *Russians Observed*. Hodder & Stoughton 1969.
Pospielovsky, D., *The Russian Church under the Soviet Regime 1917–1982*. St Vladimir's Seminary Press 1984.
Spinka, M., *The Church and the Russian Revolution*. Macmillan 1927.
Timasheff, T. S., *Religion in Soviet Russia 1917–1942*. Sheed & Ward 1943.
'The Truth about Religion in Russia', published in Russian by the Moscow Patriarchate, 1942.

Chapter Eight
The principal source for this chapter is the author's own observations, and in particular the diary of his visit to Moscow in 1943, a copy of which can be seen in the Lambeth Palace Library. See also *Sobornost*, the Journal of the Fellowship of St Alban and St Sergius, vol. 5, no. 2, pp. 46–55, 'A wartime visit to the Russian Church'; and Smyth, C., *Cyril Garbett* (1959), ch. 12.

Chapter Nine
Beeson, T., *Discretion and Valour: Religious Conditions in Russia and Eastern Europe* (2nd edn). Fount 1982.
Binyon, M., *Life in Russia* (1983).
Bourdeaux, M., *Patriarchs and Prophets: Persecution of the Russian Orthodox Church Today*. Mowbray 1975. (Valuable documents)

Bibliography

Bourdeaux, M., *Risen Indeed; Lessons in Faith from the USSR* (1983).

Bourdeaux, M., ed., *May One Believe – In Russia?: Violations of Religious Liberty in the Soviet Union.* Darton, Longman & Todd 1980.

Ellis, J., *The Russian Orthodox Church.* Croom Helm 1986.

Fletcher, W. C., *Religion and Soviet Foreign Policy, 1945–1970.* Oxford University Press 1973.

Hebly, J. A., *The Russians and the World Council of Churches.* Christian Journals 1978.

Lawrence, J., *The Hammer and the Cross.* BBC 1986.

Pascal, P., *The Religion of the Russian People.* Mowbray 1976.

The Moscow Patriarchate, 1917–1977. Moscow Patriarchate 1978.

Pitirim, Archbishop of Volokolamsk, *The Orthodox Church in Russia* (illustrated). Thames & Hudson 1982.

Pospielovsky, D., *The Russian Church under the Soviet Regime 1917–1982.* St Vladimir's Seminary Press 1984.

Struve, N., *Christians in Contemporary Russia.* Collins 1967.

Walters, P., and Balengarth, J., eds, *Light Through the Curtain.* Lion 1985.

See also Blake, E. Carson, 'East-West Relations of the WCC 1966–1972, in *Voices of Unity*, ed. van der Bent, Ans J. WCC, Geneva, 1981.

Chapter 10

The principal source for this chapter is Walter Sawatsky's comprehensive *Soviet Evangelicals since World War Two* (Herald Press, Kitchener, Ontario, 1981). There are many relevant sections in Gerhard Simon, *Church, State and Opposition in the USSR* (ed. tr. publ. C. Hurst, London, 1974). Developments in the earlier years are copiously documented in M. Bourdeaux, *Religious Ferment in Russia. Protestant Opposition to Soviet Religious Policy* (London 1968), and in many of his smaller books, e.g. *Faith on Trial in Russia* (Hodder & Stoughton, London, 1971). Georgi Vins' autobiography, *Three Generations of Suffering*, was translated by Jane Ellis and published by Hodder & Stoughton in 1976; see also Payne, E. A., *Out of Great Tribulation* (1974).

Current developments are regularly reported in the Keston College Journals, *Religion in Communist Lands, The Right to Believe*, and its other publications (address: Heathfield Road, Keston, Kent BR2 6BA); also in the English edition of the *Journal of the Moscow Patriarchate*.

References to religion in classics of Russian literature can be illuminating. For chapter 4, see the description of the staretz Zossima in Dostoevsky, *The Brothers Karamazov*, part 1, book 1, chapter 5. Tolstoy's *Anna Karenina*, part V, chapter 1, evokes the prevailing attitude to religion of educated Russians in the nineteenth century. For chapter 7, see Max Hayward, *Writers in Russian 1917–1978*, Boris Pasternak's *Doctor Zhivago* (especially the appended poems), and Alexander Solzhenitsyn's novels, *One Day in the Life of Ivan Denisovich, Cancer Ward* and *The First Circle*. See also *The Unknown Homeland*, tr. Marite Sapiéts (Mowbray 1978): the story of a priest's exile in Siberia first 'published' in Russian in *samizdat*.

Appendix 1:   The Russian Orthodox Church and the Church of England

How was it that the Archbishop of Canterbury was asked to send a representative to the coronation of the Tsar in 1896? (No other foreign Church was invited.) The first semi-official contact between the two Churches appears to have been an appeal to Moscow by the Anglican bishops who had refused to take the oath of allegiance to William and Mary in 1689 because they had already sworn obedience to King James. In 1716 they actually wrote to Peter the Great suggesting a concordat between the Russian Church and 'The Catholic Remnant' in the Church of England. Surprisingly Peter received the proposal favourably, and the Holy Synod suggested a 'friendly conference'; but Peter's death ended this initiative.

More serious attempts to build up a relationship resulted from the Anglo-Catholic revival which began in Oxford in 1833. The first advocate of a rapprochement with the Russian Church was William Palmer (1811–79) of Magdalen College, Oxford who visited Russia in 1840. He was received by Metropolitan Filaret (see page 26 above), and asked for permission to receive the Sacrament in the Orthodox Liturgy. This permission was not given, but Palmer tried to advance matters by publishing a 'Harmony of Anglican doctrine and the doctrine of the Catholic and Apostolic Church of the East'. However his views proved to be unacceptable to both English and Scottish Anglican bishops. He carried on a long exchange of letters with the philosopher-theologian Khomyakov (see page 32).

Later on other Anglicans visited the Russian Church. One was Stephen Graham who travelled extensively in Russia before 1914 and wrote several books about the Church and people. But W. J. Birkbeck, who represented the Archbishop of Canterbury at the celebrations for the nine hundredth anniversary of the Baptism of Rus in 1888, and who became a close friend of the Ober-procurator Pobedonostev and of the Tsar himself, was for many years the principal contact between Lambeth and the Holy Synod. He was responsible for visits to Moscow by Bishop Creighton in 1896 and by Archbishop Maclagan of York in 1897. Fr Walter Frere CR (afterwards Bishop of Truro) went there in 1913 and wrote a popular book called *Links in the Chain of Russian Church History*. He became the Anglican President of the Fellowship of St Alban and St Sergius (see Riley, *Birkbeck and the Eastern Church*, SPCK 1917).

Appendix 1

The Archbishop of Canterbury, Dr Randall Davidson, continued to take a close interest in the Russian Church. In September 1917 he sent a warm greeting to the newly elected national Church Council (Sobor). He was well aware of the significance of this development (see page 41). But in November the West was flooded with stories of the horrors said to be accompanying the October Revolution, and when Archbishop Davidson sent congratulations to Patriarch Tikhon on his election he referred to the difficulty and anxiety of the circumstances in which he was taking office.

At the time of the great famine in 1921 the Patriarch appealed to the Archbishop to send bread and medicines without delay. The Archbishop responded by promoting a national appeal for the Russian Famine Relief Fund. In 1922 when the news of the Patriarch's arrest was received the Archbishop spoke in the House of Lords and organized a petition to Lenin which was signed by the heads of nearly all the British Churches. When this petition was rejected as ill-informed, the Archbishop created a sensation in Russia by requesting permission to send a small body of representatives of the Churches to examine the situation and avoid future misunderstandings. Rumours flew round that the Archbishop himself had arrived in Russia. When the Soviet government again rejected the appeal and a fresh attack began on churchmen, including the Roman Catholic Metropolitan of Petrograd and his clergy, the Archbishop organized another protest, this time signed by Cardinal Bourne and the Chief Rabbi as well as the other heads of Churches. It is not known whether these moves had any effect on the Kremlin, but the Patriarch was released instead of being executed as many had feared, and he sent the Archbishop an icon. When Tikhon died in April 1925 the Archbishop sent a wreath. He was the only foreign ecclesiastic to do so.

During the next sixteen chaotic years no communications were possible between the Patriarchate and Lambeth, but Archbishop Lang supported an international protest to the Soviet government in 1931. Relations were however built up between the Church of England and various Russian Orthodox jurisdictions in the emigration, especially in Paris. Choirs of students from the Orthodox Academy there toured many English cathedrals and major churches and so gave Anglicans a precious opportunity to share in Russian liturgical worship.

In 1943 the visit of the Archbishop of York, Dr Cyril Garbett, to Moscow marked the recommencement of contacts between the Patriarchate and Churches outside the USSR. Relationships looked promising in 1945, but the rapid escalation of the Cold War soon damped these hopes. However the Moscow Conference organized by the Patriarchate in 1948 discussed the question of Anglican Orders. A resolution expressed dissatisfaction with the teaching of the Thirty-Nine Articles on the sacraments; affirmed that the question of Orders could only be settled in the context of agreement on unity of faith with the Orthodox Church, and declared that the issue must be settled by an Ecumenical Council.

The Lambeth Conference of the same year welcomed the resumption of contacts with the Russian Church, and an Anglican Theological delegation visited Moscow in 1956. The two main speakers at the conference were Bishop Michael Chub of Smolensk (1912–1985), and Dr Michael Ramsey, then Archbishop of York. The report by H. M. Waddams was published by the Faith Press in 1957.

Anglican observers were invited to attend the first Pan-Orthodox Conference at Rhodes in 1962, and at the third session in 1964 it was decided to initiate dialogue between the Orthodox Churches collectively and the Anglican Communion. Bishop (later Archbishop) Robert Runcie led a strong delegation to such an international Anglican-Orthodox Conference at Moscow in 1976, and another followed at Dublin in 1984. Thus the earlier contacts between Canterbury and Moscow have now been absorbed into the more comprehensive process of dialogue between the Churches of the Anglican Communion and the autocephalous Orthodox Churches throughout the world.

Appendix 2: Official Summary of the Rights and Obligations of Religious Societies

A religious society is formed in order to satisfy jointly religious needs and is an association of believing citizens (founding members of the society), who are of age, no less than 20 in number and reside in one district. A religious society may commence its work after it has been registered at the appropriate state bodies. This is necessary for the legality of the religious society to be recognized from the moment of registration. Moreover the registration signifies that a religious society takes upon itself the obligation of observing the USSR Constitution and the Soviet laws.

For administering the internal affairs of religious society and for economic management the meeting of the founding members must elect an executive body and an auditing commission. The executive body handles finances, signs contracts and may act as plaintiff or defendant in civil, labour and other lawsuits in which a religious society may be involved.

A religious society may invite officiants of its cult and openly hold religious services and prayer meetings in a house of worship, which may be attended by the believing citizens of any age, and perform religious rites. If the religious rites and processions have to be held outside the premises of the house of worship the permission of the Executive Committee must be obtained. Permission is not necessary if the religious rite or ceremony is a part of the religious service and takes place round the house of worship and does not violate public order or traffic rules. With the permission of the Executive Committee religious rites may be performed in the homes of citizens. Religious rites may be performed without the sanction of the Executive Committee in case of grave illness – in hospitals, in the homes for the aged and invalids, and in prisons; in case of death – at home, the cemetery or crematory. The believing citizens, including children of ten and over, may be voluntary participants in religious rites. In the case of children religious rites are performed with the consent of their parents. Religious rites have no legal force.

A religious society enjoys the rights of juridical persons and as such may, if need arises, build or purchase, with its own money and according with the law, necessary premises; acquire means of transport, church requisites, and objects of religious cult with right of ownership. The purchase by a religious society of a building for its needs is legalized by a notarized deal. The building thus acquired becomes the property of the religious society.

A religious society has a right to take a lease on property or premises. An agreement may be made with the Executive Committee for the use by a religious society of a special house of worship free of charge. For prayer meetings, a religious society may make use of other premises leased from individuals or the executive committees of a district or city Soviet of People's Deputies. A religious society may own only one house of worship.

If the house of worship, living quarters and other premises happen to be state property leased to a religious society, government insurance must be paid by the society. Furthermore, the religious society must guarantee the safety of the given property; in case of loss or damage the society will be liable. The real estate or property owned by a religious society may be insured if it so desires.

A religious society has its own monetary funds accumulated from donations and collections made in the house of worship, the sale of objects of cult and the performance of religious rites. These are free of tax. The money is spent on the upkeep of the houses of worship and other property of the cult on the wages of the servants of the cult and religious centres, as well as of workers and employees.

Possessing monetary funds, religious societies have the right to employ, on a permanent or temporary basis, workers and employees on contracts drawn up with or without trade union participation. Wages are determined by agreement with the religious societies but they must not be lower than the government rates of corresponding workers in state institutions or enterprises. Persons working for religious societies on contract drawn with the participation of a trade union are protected by labour laws. Moreover, terms of contracts drawn up by religious societies without the participation of a trade union must not in any way contradict the existing labour legislation. If they do, the contract is considered invalid.

The Journal of the Moscow Patriarchate, English Edition 1986, No. 1, p. 80.

Index

Index